www.h2so.org

About the author: Andrew Whitfield started this business purely by accident as well as from necessity. It was after a chance conversation with a good friend who was trying to sell items from a shop on eBay. He did not have a great deal of technical knowledge of how eBay and the Internet worked but enough of an understanding to list items, and he had made some sales.

Andrew, on the other hand, had never purchased or sold anything on, or even considered using, eBay, Amazon, or any other website platform to buy and sell things. He was starting as a complete beginner. Andrew has now been doing this for many years and has written a total of four books to date, and has set up an online training company. How To Sell Online Ltd (www.h2so.org) designed to help new start-ups or existing online retail business owners.

His own business sources worldwide, promotes online and ships worldwide hundreds of parcels a week. In this powerful and easy-to read book, Andrew Whitfield shows you how to make money by selling online. Find out the reality of what it takes and how your business - small or large, home-based or on the high street - can be part of it. "You may be getting started with eBay, fine-tuning your rich keywords on Amazon there's a wealth of information

Acknowledgements: In getting to the point of being able to write this and the other books which I have written it has been somewhat of a journey. Several years before writing this book I had established a business that was taking up every waking hour of my day, seven days a week. One particular day I received a mail shot from a chap by the name of Simon Coulson, I'd seen Simon a few years before so I knew there would be an upsell to me, attending an event as his guest.

I would like to thank Simon for sending that mailshot as it gave me access to some incredible people, Ben Brophy, who was given me an immense knowledge in video and photography, Raymond Aaron, who is a New York Times bestselling author and who I have worked with personally on my first book, 'How To Sell Online' he even wrote the forward for the book. I am also one of the coaches for the Internet Business School and I would like to thank all my fellow coaches for all of the input, support and information they are given to me over the years and continue to do so.

Working as a coach has enabled me to help many business owners and budding entrepreneurs and led me to set up the company How To Sell Online Ltd. (www.h2so.org) where the aim of our business is to help people either start-up their own online business or help them take their existing business to new and greater heights.

This could not have been done without the focused help and input from Elizabeth Baker, who has supported me from the very start of this journey along with my two new partners, Ben James of pureseolondon.co.uk whose knowledge of the Internet is brilliant, Jon Hepburn of the Fedora Consultancy who creates great marketing material. And of course there's my team who run the online retail business, Stuart, Mark, Taylor and headed up by Elizabeth.

The Book On How To Sell On Amazon

To Make Serious Money Online, You Need To Be There...

by

Andrew Whitfield

www.h2so.org

Copyright © 2014 Andrew Whitfield www.h2so.org

Other Books By Andrew Whitfield

- **The Book On How To Sell Online**
  - How To Make A Profit 24/7 Using The PROPEL™ Technique
- **The Book On How To Sell On EBay**
- **The Book On How To Sell On Amazon**
- **The Complete Book On How To Sell Online, EBay, Amazon & Webstore**

Copyright © 2014 Andrew Whitfield

All rights reserved

No part of this book may be reproduced in any form or by any electronic or mechanical means including information storage and retrieval systems, without permission in writing from the author. The only exception is by a reviewer, who may quote short excerpts in a published review.

The information presented herein represents the views of the author as of the date of publication. This book is presented for informational purposes only. Due to the rate at which conditions change, the author reserves the right to alter and update his opinions at any time. While every attempt has been made to verify the information in this book, the author does not assume any responsibility for errors, inaccuracies, or omissions.

CHAPTER 1 THE TOP SEVEN REASONS TO MAKE MONEY WITH AMAZON 1-9

You Need To Be There To Be Successful... 1-9
There Are Easy Ways To Start Up... 1-12
Google Yahoo And Other Search Engines Like Amazon 1-15
Customers Trust Amazon As A Trusted Brand................................. 1-17
Your Products Can Be Seen By Millions Of Potential Customers........ 1-19
Amazon Has Great Marketing Opportunities..................................... 1-20
Other People Can Sell Your Product For Free!.................................. 1-21
Take Advantage Of Great Shipping And Storage Solutions 1-23
Your Money Is Safe 1-27

CHAPTER 2 CONVERT MORE SALES IN EUROPE AND THE UNITED STATES 2-30

Why Restrict Your Market To UK Only Sales?..................................... 2-30
Sell Your Product Easily Into The European Marketplace 2-32
Language Translation Made Easy... 2-33
Sell Items Separately On Amazon.Com 2-35
Easy Ways To Overcome International Logistics 2-37
What About Cross-Border International Vat 2-38

CHAPTER 3 SYNC YOUR OTHER WEBSTORE WITH AMAZON 3-43

Easy Ways To Control Your Stock At Start-Up 3-43
Have Your Own Web Store Linked To Your Amazon Marketplace Store. 3-45
What You Can Do If You Sell On Other Platforms, EBay, Play.Com Etc. 3-47
Stock Control Made Easy With Third-Party Applications 3-50
Grow Your Business By Selling On Multiple Platforms 3-52
Setting Your Price Across Multiple Platforms 3-54

CHAPTER 4 HOW TO FIND NICHE PRODUCTS THAT SELL WITH A PROFIT 4-56

Do Your Research In Advance... 4-56

ANALYSE THE POTENTIAL NET PROFIT NET OF A PRODUCT BEFORE YOU BUY STOCK 4-62
TRADE EVENTS AND TRADE SHOWS 4-65
BUYING STOCK BY TENDER, PUBLIC, AND TRADE AUCTIONS 4-67
EASY WAYS TO FIND LIQUIDATED AND BANKRUPT STOCK 4-71
CREATE YOUR OWN BRANDED BESPOKE LABELLED PRODUCTS 4-76
HANDMADE CRAFTED AND UNIQUE PRODUCTS 4-77
HOW TO FIND END OF LINE AND CLEARANCE PRODUCTS 4-79
SOURCING PRE-OWNED OR GRADED RETURNED PRODUCTS 4-81
HOW TO BUNDLE PRODUCTS TO REDUCE COMPETITION 4-82

CHAPTER 5 THE SECRETS TO GREAT LISTINGS THAT ARE EASILY FOUND 5-85

HOW TO WRITE A GREAT PRODUCT DESCRIPTION 5-85
GIVE ACCURATE PRODUCT DIMENSIONS 5-87
HOW TO USE AMAZON BULLET POINTS 5-88
HOW TO USE BRILLIANT PHOTOGRAPHY 5-90
OFFER FAST AND FREE DELIVERY OPTIONS 5-91
ASK CUSTOMERS FOR REVIEWS OF YOUR PRODUCT 5-94

CHAPTER 6 GREAT TITLES THAT SELL MORE OF YOUR PRODUCTS ... 6-96

WHY IS THE TITLE SO IMPORTANT? 6-96
HAVE A KEYWORD STRATEGY THAT WORKS 6-98
HOW TO FIND SHORT AND LONG TAIL KEYWORDS 6-99

CHAPTER 7 HOW TO USE THE SEASONALITY CHECKLIST 7-102

SOME POSITIVE EFFECTS CHANGING THE KEYWORDS IN YOUR TITLES CAN HAVE .. 7-102
THE BEST WAY TO MANAGE THE SEASONAL FLUCTUATIONS 7-103
HOW TO EFFECTIVELY MANAGE THE SEASONAL PLAN 7-105
EASY WAYS TO PLAN YOUR STOCK LEVELS 7-106
KNOW YOUR DEMOGRAPHICS 7-108

CHAPTER 8 HOW TO USE AMAZON MARKETING STRATEGIES TO CONVERT MORE SALES 8-110

WHAT IS THE RIGHT STRATEGY FOR YOU 8-110

CREATE HUGE DISCOUNTS WITH SALE PRICES 8-112
YOU CAN CREATE MARKETING CAMPAIGNS 8-113
USE FULFILMENT BY AMAZON OPPORTUNITIES 8-114
YOU CAN USE AMAZON PRODUCT ADVERTS 8-115

CHAPTER 9 CREATE 'WOW' FACTOR VISIBILITY, CREDIBILITY AND FEEDBACK 9-118

THE CUSTOMER IS ALWAYS RIGHT! 9-118
MANAGE YOUR CUSTOMER'S EXPECTATIONS UNDER PROMISE AND OVER DELIVER
.... 9-119
   Personalise Your Email Replies *9-122*
MAKE YOURSELF VISIBLE TO THE CUSTOMER 9-125
HOW TO CONTROL FREQUENTLY ASKED QUESTIONS 9-126
ISSUES WILL ARISE, SO FIX THEM 9-128
RESPOND TO ALL NEGATIVE FEEDBACK 9-130
YOU HAVE AN A-Z CASE 9-133

CHAPTER 10 HOW TO UNDERSTAND YOUR AMAZON SELLER RATINGS AND METRICS 10-136

STAY FIT AND HEALTHY AS A SELLER 10-136
GREEN TICKS AND RED CROSSES 10-138
KNOW THE AMAZON POLICIES 10-139
LOOK OUT FOR POLICY VIOLATION 10-140
WHAT CAN YOU SELL ON AMAZON 10-141
YOU MIGHT NOT BE ABLE TO SELL TOYS AT CHRISTMAS 10-142

CHAPTER 11 FIND EASY AND COST-EFFECTIVE WAYS TO SHIP YOUR ITEMS 11-144

HOW DO I COST EFFECTIVELY SHIP ITEMS 11-144
SIMPLE STEPS TO GET YOUR SHIPPING OFF TO A FINE START 11-145

CHAPTER 12 BONUS CHAPTER: THE GOLDEN RULES TO GUARANTEE SUCCESS SELLING ON AMAZON 12-150

BE AN HONEST SELLER 12-150
HOW TO STAY CUSTOMER FOCUSED 12-151
THE VALUE OF A WELL-WRITTEN EMAIL 12-152

BE ACCURATE IN YOUR PRODUCT LISTINGS 12-154
REACT TO NEGATIVE FEEDBACK POSITIVELY 12-155
DO NOT TAKE CRITICISM PERSONALLY 12-155
UNDERSTAND AMAZON WANT YOU TO SUCCEED TOO 12-156
KNOW YOUR METRICS, RATINGS AND AREAS OF IMPROVEMENT 12-158
DELIVERING GREAT SERVICE ON TIME 12-159

CHAPTER 13 BONUS PAGE: FIVE INCREDIBLE BONUSES TO MAKE YOUR BUSINESS GROW 13-161

FREE TOP 10 AMAZON MISTAKES AND HOW TO AVOID THEM REPORT 13-161
FREE CHAPTER OF THE BOOK ON HOW TO SELL ON EBAY 13-161
FREE 20 MINUTE INVITATION FOR A TELEPHONE CONSULTATION WITH THE AUTHOR 13-161
ONE HALF-PRICE WORKSHOP OF YOUR CHOICE 13-161
THE OPPORTUNITY TO TAKE ADVANTAGE SIX MONTHS FREE MEMBERSHIP TO HOW TO SELL ONLINE WHEN PURCHASING AN ANNUAL MEMBERSHIP PACKAGE 13-161

Chapter 1 The Top Seven Reasons To Make Money With Amazon

You Need To Be There To Be Successful

For those of you that have read 'The Book On How To Sell Online' you will be aware that I started the online business out of necessity as a means to earn money and to live a great lifestyle. In the many years since I started the online retail business I have turned over many millions of pounds, created jobs and employment and also given back to good causes.

I could not have done any of this if I hadn't used the Amazon marketplace platform, this is where I have made the greatest amount of turnover and when I measure it against eBay, standalone web shops, play.com and the other various retail methods I've used to sell products, it has represented some 68% of my total turnover. Now that is a big number when you consider the amount of turnover I have generated since I started.

In those early days it was down to myself and my partner to purchase the stock, I would write the sales page for the item, I would take my own photographs, I would list the item, I would deal with the customer service enquiries both by email and telephone, every morning I would compile a spreadsheet of the orders to print the mailing labels.

My partner would then pick the items that had been sold pack them to the high standard that I insisted upon before posting them to the purchaser and sending them an email to confirm that they had been dispatched.

Those days were great days, and busy peak times such as Christmas, Valentine's Day, Mother's Day and Father's Day they could also be stressful times. To run a very successful online or off-line retail business you need to be focused and prepared to roll your sleeves up and get stuck into the work that is required to meet the your customer's expectations and deadlines. A present or gift delivered late does not have the same appeal as one delivered on time.

Those were as they say 'the good old days' I now have a great team of people around me, 99% of the products we sell are now sent from third-party fulfilment centres or direct from our suppliers, I have invested in technology, infrastructure, people and most importantly I have invested time and effort in my own education and personal development.

That does not mean that I have not made mistakes along the way, I have. The mistakes that I have made I have learnt from and form part of the reason that I wrote 'The Book On

How To Sell Online' and have set up a training company **www.h2so.org** (How To Sell Online Ltd) so that I and my team can assist other business owners and budding entrepreneurs to create great businesses, achieve their goals and personal financial freedom.

Every week you can pick up on the news channels throughout the world that online retail is growing and growing and growing. Therefore, if you are an independent retailer where does this leave you in the great Internet haystack?

Lots of people will set up a small retail website, sit back and think that it I've made it I've got an online shop I am going to make my fortune. The reality is somewhat different, you have got to put some time and effort in getting your online retail business up and running and established.

In today's market that means you have to be using platforms such as Amazon, Google, eBay to name but three. You need to look at their power and dominance of the Internet's marketplace. If you type a search term into your web browser because you want to purchase a product the chances are that Amazon will have a match on that search on page 1 of the search engine (according to some recent statistics Google has over 90% of the search traffic in our retail marketplace). So as we see independent retailers seeing their sales slide and their page ranking diminish it is time that they took a fresh look at the marketplaces that are available to them. That is why you need to be there, to be on Amazon if you want to be successful and make money selling products online.

There Are Easy Ways To Start Up

If you are new to selling online then the easiest way to start up is to go out purchase products and create a few listings on Amazon using their basic entry-level subscription. Amazon have a very interactive website so you will never get stuck and never be more than a click or a phone call away from their customer service team that can give you help and advice.

As part of growing the business I have hit various hurdles that I've needed to overcome, I cannot speak highly enough or recommend strongly enough that you contact Amazons merchant seller helpline. Amazon is a very customer focused organisation, I do come across a number of people that say Amazon is focused only at the end user customer (i.e. the purchaser of a product), from my experience that is totally incorrect because as a retail marketplace merchant selling on Amazon I am also an Amazon customer.

As an Amazon customer I am generating part of the income that makes Amazon the great place to shop that it is today.

So whenever I have had hurdles to get over the Amazon customer service team have been excellent at delivering the answer. Now the answer may not always be the one that I want or it may be that I cannot do it in the way that I wanted to, but I have been given an answer and I have been given a way in which I can do what is required.

Therefore you have got to have the flexibility and the mindset to accept that you may have to do things differently and you may have to comply to rules and regulations that you personally do not agree with.

If you already have an inventory, you are an existing retail business online or off-line then you can upload your inventory very easily into Amazon. When I first started I used to list each item individually until I got to know the system, once I was comfortable with their system I used their spreadsheet templates.

Their templates look very daunting if you're not used to using spreadsheets, however sitting down with a good cup of coffee you will soon start to realise that the spreadsheets just follow a logical pattern and once you have established the pattern your mindset will change and you will be able to upload your data from any existing spreadsheet you have using very simple copy and paste functions onto the Amazon spreadsheets.

One of the best things about using the spreadsheet method is that if you do upload the spreadsheet incorrectly you will have an error report from Amazon. That error report will tell you exactly what you need to change and normally within a few clicks those changes can be made and your products are live.

As I said earlier when you get an error report if it doesn't make sense contact Amazon customer support, they will be able to talk you through it. I have done this a number of times when I've had very large multiple spreadsheets to upload and even now my team will ask questions when we are listing a product that might have specific variations that require more in-depth understanding of how the spreadsheet will interpret or display the data.

This is one of the reasons that I set up **www.h2so.org** as I am frequently asked questions on how to complete tasks so we offer workshops and one-to-one mentoring based on our experience to assist people who are serious about selling online and in particular Amazon.

As you become more confident in your skills of using Amazon you can obviously upgrade to one of their other packages and become a pro merchant seller.

Success *Tip*:

When you register with Amazon and you are creating a merchant shop you will be asked to provide a shop name, if you have an existing web store or thinking of expanding to a web store then you should ensure that the name of your shop is the same as or at least as near to that trading name as possible. You will not be allowed to use the prefix www. or suffix .com, .co.uk etc.

If you have not secured your web shop domain names it may be a good idea to do so at this point to ensure that they are still available for you to use so that you can expand into your web store when you are ready. Great place to obtain domain names are 1and1, GoDaddy, 123reg or search online for domain registrations.

Google Yahoo And Other Search Engines Like Amazon

Whenever I'm researching new products to sell I will always put the product title, importers or manufacturers title, the barcode and other keyword data into Google so that I can see where my competition is in the marketplace and whether the product is profitable enough to be a sustainable online selling item.

Using Pareto's principle of the 80/20 rule, I can guarantee that if the product is already available to consumers that I will find it listed on page 1 of Google with a link back to Amazon. And again using the same principle there is a really high percentage chance that if the seller on Amazon is also selling on their own independent web store that they do not appear on the first three pages of Google.

Such is the power of trading on Amazon as they have massive resources and are consistently liked by the search engines as they are a trusted source of data to the keywords that have been entered into the search engines search box.

I was preparing for one of my workshops and to prove this point I searched for a particular item on Google, an imported campervan clock, I put the search words 'miniature blue campervan clock' into the Google search box and it returned several pages of matches. Amazon dominated the top five listings, eBay was also on the first page, the web store of the company selling the item was not on the first three pages of Google and at that point I did not look any further.

This goes to show the power of Amazon and how Amazon can get your products, if correctly listed with current and relevant keyword strategies (which are covered in a later chapter) onto page one of the most powerful search engine in the world.

Now do you want to be found on page 1 of Google and is it worth the seller fee that you will pay to Amazon? I certainly think it is.

Customers Trust Amazon As A Trusted Brand

There is no doubt about it Amazon is a brand, yes it started by selling online books but now you can buy everything from books, DVD's, washing machines, televisions, clothing, chocolate, hampers, groceries virtually anything.

This is due to Amazon being totally customer focused, Amazon have a very straightforward customer service policy in that if a customer is unhappy fix it to make them happy. Now there are exceptions to every rule, some customers are unscrupulous. Amazon and all the other platforms take on board that some customers may not always be totally honest. Where this happens and there is enough evidence to show that this is the case those customers will normally have their accounts restricted or removed.

Therefore, if you are serious about selling on Amazon or any of these platforms you must be very customer focused. If you are not customer focused, do not want to follow the rules under the distant selling regulations in the UK, Europe or other countries then I suggest you do not get involved in online retail.

It is because companies like Amazon are so customer focused that they are so successful and people return many times over to make repeat purchases. If your product is a consumable product that a customer would order on a regular basis then giving them great customer service they will keep coming back to you time and time again. On the other hand if your purchase is transaction led but the customer receives excellent customer service there is a greater chance that they will recommend your products to friend's colleagues and relations.

To be part of a trusted brand you need to be fully focused on delivering excellent customer service, replying to emails quickly, answering questions, dealing with issues when they arise, embracing customer return policies and going that extra mile to deliver total satisfaction when it's required.

One of the things to bear in mind that when customers contact you is that very often they do not understand or have a grasp of how Amazon works or is structured. Therefore in our office we very often receive phone calls from customers who are rather surprised to be answered personally by one of my team and will very often ask, "Is that Amazon?" How great is that!

Your Products Can Be Seen By Millions Of Potential Customers

Not only are your products being brought to the front pages of Google and the other search engines but obviously people also search within Amazon itself, now although Amazon.co.uk is seen as trading in the UK only people look on Amazon from all over the world, so we have customers where we send items out to Australia, Russia, Europe, New Zealand almost anywhere.

Because of the way Amazon has built up its worldwide reputation it means that people use Amazon from other countries or they may be expats, overseas workers or have spent time within the UK. This means Amazon is their point of reference when they wish to make a purchase, we have customers that have purchased items from us in the UK and have them shipped out to the country that we originally imported them from! Now that is the power of having your product listed on such a great platform.

Maybe you do not want to sell to those people outside of the UK and you only want to sell your products on the UK mainland. If you have really strong reasons for doing so then fair enough. But, you are missing out on millions of searches carried out on Amazon every day for products that people will purchase outside of the UK.

Amazon Has Great Marketing Opportunities

As online retailing continues to grow throughout the UK and worldwide it is becoming ever more competitive, Amazon have recently created some great new marketing strategies for the retail sector, so you can offer things like:

- free shipping
- next day or expedited shipping
- guaranteed next day delivery
- buy one get one free/half-price/other discount
- sales price strategies that can be pre-set in advance
- Amazon's own pay per click options

Amazon are very keen for you to sell more product and have been developing tools that you can take full advantage of in promoting your products, multiple product sales, discounts.

If you are going to take advantage of using the Amazon marketing opportunities one of the things you need to do is to be clear about your pricing, the net return you require from the product that you are selling, what your competitors strategy will be, and to ensure that it is sustainable for the period of time the marketing promotion is available.

Using any of their various strategies is great especially if you are selling seasonal products or you are targeting markets such as Valentine's Day, Halloween, Mother's Day where you only have one shot at selling your stock and making a profit from that event.

If you are going to use these strategies to get them ready several weeks in advance in order for price discounts to legally come into effect or for your promotion to be featured through the search engines by additional marketing strategies such as pay per click campaigns.

Other People Can Sell Your Product For Free!

Another great way to drive sales and unless you're in the Internet marketing arena you may never have come across this before, is through affiliates.

Amazon allow other people to become an affiliate which basically means they will market your product for you, without your knowledge, and every sale that the affiliate makes of your product attracts a commission that is paid by Amazon to them directly. That is great isn't it!

An affiliate will actively promote your product through blogs and possibly directly to customer lists, when an affiliate markets your product the link that they use to your Amazon product contains some special html code that identifies the affiliate as being the person who has introduced the customer to your product to make the purchase.

The best bit is that Amazon are paying the affiliate a commission and it has no impact on you other than you sell more.

Now good affiliate marketers are only looking for good products that are either going to give them a high return or they can attract volume sales which will give them a good return. Normally it is a short run so you will get a spike in your sales and you may have no particular reason for seeing such a spike. So to attract the affiliate marketers, have good quality products that have got a good return, if the affiliate's marketing to a large email list they may be looking for volume sales from good quality listings with good keyword strategies.

There are opportunities for you to offer your own affiliation strategies if you have your own web store which has a data capture systems such as Aweber or Marketers Choice/One Shopping Cart. If you're not familiar with the systems then it would be worth spending a little time to research them online.

Take Advantage Of Great Shipping And Storage Solutions

Whether you are starting out or you're already selling online one of the great considerations you have to make is storage of your stock. Then you've got to get into the routine of picking packing or posting in dealing with all customer service issues that may go with sending your stock at.

When you are only sending 20 parcels at the time then that is fairly manageable once you start getting to the point where you're sending out 40 or more then it becomes a time issue in your daily routine. It is always better to prepare for the increase in sales by exploring your options to get more help.

You could look at obtaining help from a member of the family or close friend which will probably help you out over the initial period of time but of course they also have their own lives to lead and it may not always be convenient for them to help you out.

With Amazon you do have another option, Amazon call it 'FBA', which stands for "Fulfilment by Amazon", this is a really great service to use, however, you do have to be organised and I will deal with that in a little bit more detail.

The FBA principle works on the basis that you list your items on Amazon as normal and you then change the listing from being fulfilled by you, once Amazon have received it and confirm that it is on their system, by switching it to Amazon fulfilled.

This means the physical listing of your item does not change it is purely one part of the listing that will be changed to a different setting. So this is a very easy process to follow. We have used Amazon fulfilment services and for us we found the best way to ensure that there was no interruption in sales was to retain a quantity for ourselves and send a partial amount of the stock to Amazon for them to fulfil directly.

It can take Amazon up to 10 days to book your items in so there is always that potential time lag where you could be losing sales if you don't retain some stock yourself. Every item you list on Amazon will have a unique code called an ASIN reference and you will also have your unique 13 digit EAN number (more commonly known as a barcode). The requirement Amazon has is that you label correctly the items you send to them with either your EAN number (barcode) along with your SKU code which is your unique stock item reference number.

For Amazon to book the items in they must be able to read those barcodes with their scanners and of course every item inside a box needs to also have those barcodes attached to them so that they can be identified individually. So there is a little bit of work for you to do before you send the product but once it has gone and they have received it you can sit back and watch your sales grow. You can watch the money coming in knowing that Amazon are doing the pick, pack and postage for you.

There are also a number of other benefits to using Amazon's FBA service, Amazon will charge you a small fee for storage based on the actual space the product will take up on the shelf, also you're taking advantage of Amazon's massive purchasing power.

- Packaging; Amazon go through thousands of boxes and packaging materials, therefore their purchase power from their supply chain is massive and you reap the benefits of that in low-cost packaging.
- Postage; this is the biggest area that you will save money, Amazon send out millions of parcels worldwide everyday their contracts are with all the major couriers and of course they have negotiated contracts at such a price that you and I would never be able to compete.
    - UK mainland postage is extremely competitive using Amazon's fulfilment services and if you are just starting out you will be able to compare their posting services by looking at their tables against Royal Mail, Parcel2Ship, Parcel2Go, City Link, DHL, Yodel, to name but a few.

- One of the biggest advantages for you as a seller on Amazon is that you can now ship to European countries at fixed rates. Amazon's infrastructure and technology has meant that they can dispatch orders from the UK to one of their European hubs overnight and then dispatch your products to the customer.
- This makes European selling through Amazon massively advantageous, you do not have the cost of shipping the products at an uncompetitive price, you can target the European market knowing that the customer is going to get their products delivered relatively quickly and cost effectively because of Amazon's infrastructure.

There are some downsides to using the fulfilment service, you cannot cross market your product to your customer unless you have put marketing material into the products you send Amazon before they have been shipped to the fulfilment centre.

You are handing your customer service over to Amazon and they will have the final input in the majority of cases as to whether a customer returns an item for a refund, you may have opted to negotiate a discount with the buyer in order to satisfy their requirements.

If an item is returned to Amazon, it will be deemed as non-saleable and you will have the option of paying Amazon to either destroy it or return it back to you. If an item is returned, Amazon will not put it back on the shelf as a saleable item.

So before using Amazon fulfilment services it is a good idea to look at the product that you're selling and to ensure that it is suitable to meet the requirements of the service and to also ensure that you are going to be happy with a potential greater number of returns. You should also look at this from the positive point of view that you will have an increase in sales as a number of the Amazon customers will be guaranteed next day free shipping.

Your Money Is Safe

Every two weeks I receive a bank transmission from Amazon for the value of my sales for that two-week period, less any credits or refunds that have been applied and of course less any seller fees and subscriptions.

Some people may not be happy with receiving money every two weeks and would rather have instant transactions, then Amazon is not for you. However you money is safe with Amazon you haven't got to worry about credit card fraud, you haven't got to worry about credit card processing and processing fees, it is all taken care of for you by Amazon.

Now unless you are going to give massive unconditional warranties on products you will find the transmission will happen seamlessly and automatically without fail. I have never had a problem with a transmission reaching my bank account.

There may be occasions when you have a seasonal or unexpected massive spike in sales that Amazon was not expecting or you are going to offer long-term unconditional money back warranties on products, if that is the case Amazon may place money into a reserve fund, which you will be able to see on your dashboard, until such time as you have managed to provide them with additional information or your unconditional warranty has expired. All major credit card companies operate on this basis. So Best practice is not to have long or unconditional warranties.

This happened to me one Christmas where they withheld several thousands of pounds which represented a high proportion of the sales for that two-week period. Our sales had spiked very quickly in a very short period of time on a particular product range, it was their way of checking that we weren't doing anything fraudulently. The money was held up for approximately 2 weeks after they were given additional information regarding the high spike in sales.

So with Amazon you can sell with confidence, you do not have to have your own credit card merchant ID, you do not have to do worry about processing transactions and credit card fraud, you can sit back relax and watch your account balance growing in complete confidence that it will be transferred to your bank every two weeks.

Chapter 2 Convert More Sales In Europe And The United States

Why Restrict Your Market To UK Only Sales?

I have seen our sales increase dramatically across all of our platforms throughout the world, when I speak to other online retailers, who like myself have gone down the route of selling internationally, they are on the whole having the same results. The best bit is there is very little if any extra work to be done to capture the sales and the customer is more than happy to pay the additional postage.

I also hear from the naysayers that they cannot trust the post, what happens if it gets lost, what happens if the customer order to return it, what happens if...

But what happens if, also happens in the UK, you need to evaluate the business case for sending your products out of the UK. We have sent china, resin, tiles and all sorts of fragile breakable items around the world. The profit return on these products has been greater than the number breakages or the number of losses. My experience is that I can command better profit margins in selling my items overseas and have no more issues than I would selling them only in the UK.

Most countries have a relatively good postal system, for those countries who do not have a brilliant postal system then you may look at using signed for delivery by a contract courier company. The European and international market is growing massively and you need to be there to be able to command some good profits.

On the flip side of that, the international market for people sending product into the UK directly to consumers is also growing, so if you are one of the naysayers that sells mainstream products imported to the UK then you may find that your market is being attacked from international sellers. So if you have products that are price competitive and sensitive you need to be fully aware that the international sellers from competing countries are targeting the UK market. It may be you need to re-evaluate your product lines and your mindset.

As an example we had a customer that purchased two Barbie body boards from us at a total cost of £36 and then went on to pay £109.00 to have them shipped to Brazil by UPS. So if you're in the mindset that the postage is too expensive I can tell you now that you need to change your position. I have numerous examples where people have paid postage costs of more than the cost of the item to have them sent internationally.

Sell Your Product Easily Into The European Marketplace

Using Amazon's fulfilment service you have got a really cost-effective route to market to sell into Europe. Postage packing and handling charges are extremely competitive and you are taking advantage, as already stated earlier, of the massive discounts that of the negotiated by Amazon.

In the main European countries you are adding no more than 1 to 2 days onto standard delivery for a UK customer. The item doesn't even leave the UK until the purchase has been confirmed. So you don't even have to do split your stock into various different European warehouses. Amazon really have got a fantastic European offering that cannot be beaten by any other fulfilment house in the current marketplace.

When you open your online shop in the UK, you will also have the option to open your shops in the competing European countries (DE = Germany, FR = France etc. Check Amazon for its full list of countries).

When you opt to sell your products in one of the European countries this means you are listed on that platform for that country (as indicated above). Think about this for a moment, if your product has a lot of competition in the UK but very little competition in France where you know that it would sell relatively well, what restrictions are you putting on yourself in not allowing that product to be sold in France on Amazon's French website!

This is such a major opportunity for you to sell products in new and emerging marketplaces, you do not have to worry about exchange rates, or collecting the money as Amazon deal with all this for you.

You have a massive opportunity to take your products to any of the European sites and be ahead of your competition and increase your sales dramatically. Assuming you do this correctly and you are using Amazon fulfilment services all you have to do is ensure that they have always got stock from your suppliers to fulfil the orders that are coming from your customers.

Language Translation Made Easy

They have thought of that too, language translation is relatively straightforward these days there are a number of pieces of software that will translate the text for you on an automated basis. Amazon will also offer translation services and they are worth investigating and following up.

My personal view, is that if I have a product that is of high value with good profit potential I would sooner outsource to a third party language translator for my main title, description and bullet points. This way I am getting an accurate translation where I can instruct the outsourcer to deal with any specific local dialect which may be missed on an automated translation.

To do this there is a cost, so you need to do your market research first and ensure that the product has good amount of profitability. I tend to use the services of fiverr.com, elance.com or Odesk.com. With these websites you can look for or post jobs on to the website and get quotes from people to carry out the translation. With all of these sites you can actually look at their feedback for work they've done for other people in the past so you can get a good idea of how reliable they are.

If your product has a low value to it and a fairly low return then you may be quite happy using standard language translation software, however, please ensure that you monitor feedback or questions from customers to identify any areas where there may be some ambiguity.

Success Tip: you will receive customer enquiries in different languages, subscribe to and use one of the translation tools available on Google so that you can understand the question and send your reply in the language that it has been sent to you by using that translation tool.

It is also advisable to put a disclaimer at the bottom of your email that states, in their language, that you have used a translation tool to review the customer's question and to translate your reply. This then avoids any embarrassment if part of the translation has been lost.

Sell Items Separately On Amazon.Com

If you are wanting to sell your items on Amazon.com in the United States then you will have to open a separate account and upload your listings separately from your.co.uk Amazon account.

At the time of writing Amazon's European sites cannot automatically migrate to Amazon.com. Therefore you need to add Amazon.com as a separate selling channel. This is relatively easy to achieve if you've uploaded everything to Amazon on spreadsheet format. You should be able to collate the majority of the data from the spreadsheet you have used for.co.uk and transfer it onto the template sheets for Amazon.com by simply copy and paste.

Assuming you sell products that the American market has a desire for this will become a very lucrative for you and is worth spending the time creating targeted keyword rich listings on the .com site.

All of the other principals about selling on Amazon are identical, you will still be paid every two weeks, your money is still safe, you will be paid in dollars but it will be converted into your preferred currency.

You will need to put your prices in dollars and work out your shipping costs in dollars, if your items are going to attract import duty for the customer you will need to decide how you will deal with that and ensure that that is clearly stated in the description or condition note of the item listed.

The market in the United States more mature than the UK market and you would be very well advised to do some market research before selling your products to the US. If you have a mainstream product that is highly competitive and already freely available over there you may not be able to compete. If your product is a niche item and is highly desirable then you have a great marketplace and you may be able to command greater profit margins due to its desirability.

Easy Ways To Overcome International Logistics

If you are looking at using Amazon fulfilment services then you can still do this even in the US. You have the opportunity to export your product to fulfilment services in the US both with Amazon or independently to other fulfilment companies which are more advanced than the UK.

If you are a direct importer into the UK then it may be that you split your product delivery accordingly and have your items imported directly into the United States and forwarded to the fulfilment house ready for immediate dispatch directly to a customer

You may decide to hold the items yourself and use various Courier services to collect from you directly and export them accordingly, there are a number of companies who specialise in one-off or small volume shipments, Parcel2Go, Parcel2Ship, Worldwide Parcel Services, Parcelforce, DHL, UPS to name but a few. The majority of these services will have your product air born within 24 hours and will add 2 to 3 days additional shipping time to what you would expect to see a standard in the UK.

What About Cross-Border International Vat

Cross-border sales in Europe are set to continue to grow massively year on year according to IMRG (IMRG is the UK's industry association for online retail). Many retailers are expanding to new regions which means they must keep a number of important factors such VAT at the forefront of their expansion plans. However, keeping on top of changing VAT rates, distance selling thresholds and country specific information can seem like a full time job. To assist you further we have attached the EU and worldwide VAT threshold table, please be aware this was correct at time of publication of this document and we strongly suggest you check the how HMRC government or European Union websites for more recent updates.

Don't let VAT be a deterrent to your international expansion plans by making yourself aware of the individual requirements of each country you can expand comfortable in the knowledge that you are compliant. We strongly suggest that you take proper advice from a qualified accountant, VAT tax expert or contact your local VAT office for further assistance

Know the distance selling thresholds for different countries each EU Member State has a distance selling threshold, which is essentially a turnover threshold ranging between €35,000 and €100,000. Distance selling occurs when a retailer sells a product (e.g. over the internet, by telephone or by mail order) and delivers this from one EU Member State to a customer in another. If a seller exceeds the turnover threshold in an EU Member State, they will have a liability to VAT register there and charge the relative local VAT rate on their sales. For that reason it is essential that vendors who are distance selling are aware of these thresholds.

Make sure your invoices comply with local legislation if a retailer exceeds the distance selling threshold and registers for VAT in another EU country, they will need to make sure their invoices comply with local legislation. Most EU Member States legally require an invoice to be issued for distance sellers. Policy made at an EU level intended for invoices to be the same across the board in the EU, however, in reality this is not the case and there are many specific deviations. Distance sellers should understand the nuances of each country and comply with these requirements.

Know the correct VAT rates for the countries where you sell as a retailer you are probably aware of the complications that can arise from the various VAT rates which apply in your own country. This involves determining whether the standard, reduced or zero rates should be charges on a product-often not as straightforward as you might expect. Now retailers selling across the EU must apply the correct VAT rate on sales in other EU Member States. VAT rates across these countries can differ widely.

Sellers should ensure that they apply the correct VAT rate to their products. For example, books in Romania are sold with the standard VAT rate, in Ireland they are exempt from VAT altogether.

Get to know what intrastat declarations are - and submit them. Many distance sellers are totally unaware of Intrastat declarations. Following a VAT registration in another EU country, many retailers will be required to submit intrastat declarations too. The turnover thresholds for Intrastat vary within the EU, and can range from €700 to €900,000. Non-compliance in this area can also lead to penalties and fines being levied on the seller.

Private sellers on marketplaces can be liable for VAT too as e-commerce has grown, the number of private individuals selling items on channels such as eBay and Amazon has increased. As these sellers do not consider themselves to be companies, many do not take into consideration their potential VAT registration liability in their own Member State, or indeed in any other. A private seller in Germany was recently found to be liable to VAT register due to the volumes of turnover accrued through online sales on eBay. The range of goods, the manner in which they were displayed, and the product descriptions were in line with those of VAT registered sellers.

The result was that the German VAT Administration deemed that as the turnover threshold for a domestic seller had been exceeded, VAT must be declared on the sales of the good. The same applies to small businesses and private vendors selling into other European countries. Once the distance seller threshold has been exceeded, a VAT registration in that Member State will be necessary. If in doubt, better to have it checked out.

Make your webstore VAT friendly since your webstore is an important platform for online sales, it is important that it is set up for international e-commerce. This means it should be capable of showing different currencies and the relevant VAT rate that will be applied on the product. Consumer Protection Laws within the EU require that before a consumer purchases a good, the full selling pricing, including VAT, packaging and transportation be shown clearly before placing the order.

The annexe threshold table on the next page was correct at the time of printing.

Source: http://ec.europa.eu/taxation_customs/

ANNEX 1: THRESHOLDS (MARCH 2012)

Member State	Threshold for application of the special scheme for acquisitions by taxable persons not entitled to deduct input tax and by non-taxable legal persons[1]		Threshold for application of the special scheme for distance selling[2]		Exemption for small enterprises[3]	
	National currency	Euro equivalent	National currency	Euro equivalent	National currency	Euro equivalent
Belgium	€11.200	-	€35.000	-	€5.580	-
Bulgaria	20.000 BGN	10.226	70.000 BGN	35.791	50.000 BGN	25.565
Czech Republic	326.000 CZK	13.318	1.140.000 CZK	46.570	1.000.000 CZK	40.851
Denmark	80.000 DKK	10.730	280.000 DKK	37.557	50.000 DKK	6.707
Germany	€12.500	-	€100.000	-	€17.500	-
Estonia	€10.226	-	€35.151	-	€15.978	-
Ireland	€41.000	-	€35.000	-	€75.000 or €37.500	-
Greece	€10.000	-	€35.000	-	€10.000 or €5.000	-
Spain	€10.000	-	€100.000	-	None	None
France	€10.000	-	€100.000	-	€81.500 or €32.600	-
Italy	€10.000	-	€35.000	-	€30.000	-
Cyprus	€10.251	-	€35.000	-	€15.600	-
Latvia	7.000 LVL	9.932	24.000 LVL	34.052	35.000 LVL	49.659
Lithuania	35.000 LTL	10.137	125.000 LTL	36.203	100.000 LTL	28.962
Luxembourg	€10.000	-	€100.000	-	€10.000	-
Hungary	2.500.000 HUF	9.164	8.800.000 HUF	32.257	5.000.000 HUF	18.328
Malta	€10.000	-	€35.000	-	€35.000 or €24.000 or €14.000	-
Netherlands	€10.000	-	€100.000	-	None	None
Austria	€11.000	-	€35.000	-	€30.000	-
Poland	50.000 PLN	12.592	160.000 PLN	40.293	150.000 PLN	37.774
Portugal	€10.000	-	€35.000	-	€10.000 or €12.500	-
Romania	34.000 RON	8.071	118.000 RON	28.012	119.000 RON	28.249
Slovenia	€10.000	-	€35.000	-	€25.000	-
Slovakia	€13.941,45	-	€35.000	-	€49.790	-
Finland	€10.000	-	€35.000	-	€8.500	-
Sweden	90.000 SEK	10.190	320.000 SEK	36.232	None	None
United Kingdom	70.000 GBP	81.843	70.000 GBP	81.843	70.000 GBP	81.843

Chapter 3 Sync Your Other Webstore With Amazon

Easy Ways To Control Your Stock At Start-Up

When you first start up your online business you may go out and buy 10 items of stock to sell and that becomes relatively easy to manage, as you sell one you can physically see you have nine left and as they start decreasing you can either go and purchase more of the same or diversify into different products.

As you grow your business with multiple lines of stock, increase the amount of stock that you hold and you are looking to sell through a number of different platforms you will need to put some form of stock management in place.

In the very early days most people will start off with a manual ledger or an Excel spreadsheet and will just edit the quantity available as the sales trickle in. This was the way that I started many years ago, a spreadsheet and a visual indication that when I got stock to as low as two products left I would look at either purchasing more or if they were end of line products that I'd sold I would look at which the platform it was selling the quickest and I would delete it off the slower moving platforms.

As time goes on and stock grows this becomes a greater and more difficult task.

Amazon has come up with a rather smart solution to help people who have independent web stores that are currently trading by allowing you to link your web store into your Amazon account.

This is very clever as it allows you to list the item on your own website alongside your Amazon.co.uk shop and if you're selling into Europe through one of the European sites it will link up to those sites as well.

The clever bit is this means you just have to have one inventory listing with one stock entry. Therefore if you purchase 10 items of stock you will show on your Amazon stock inventory 10 items, this means if you sell one item in your web store, two items in your Amazon UK marketplace, and two items on your Amazon European listings it will allocate the stock accordingly and the stock figure available would show five as you have had five sales.

This means you do not have to worry about your stock control, you can leave Amazon to do that for you. This is a very smart and clever technique provided by Amazon.

Have Your Own Web Store Linked To Your Amazon Marketplace Store

As I have already stated above by linking your web store to your Amazon marketplace account you can effectively deal with issues of stock management (if you are selling on other platforms like eBay or play.com you would have to make manual adjustments across the platforms).

Amazon will charge you a monthly subscription free to host your shop and you would need to move your existing domain name from its current hosting service to Amazon's hosting service by changing the DNS settings. This may be something you would ask your web designer to do for you. Be aware that if you are doing this and you pay your web designer and annual fee for hosting that you will be saving that fee.

The one small drawback for any small business in transferring their web shop is that you have got to transfer or re-list all of your items and you may have to do to some design work to get the shop to look and feel how you want it. So that may be an element of cost in both time and money, depending on how long your site is down and how complex it is to upload your products and any variations so you may have a period of zero sales.

Therefore to transfer your existing web store onto Amazon's platform should not be undertaken lightly, and you should always choose a time of year where sales are relatively quiet so that you do not have any major interruption to your cash flow.

Having dealt with the down side, the upside is brilliant insofar as your inventory management is purely through Amazon and no longer an issue. If you have just started out and you currently have no credit card facilities or your credit card facilities are rather expensive, then you will find that Amazon will take care of the money for you and is competitive. So again you have safety in knowing that every two weeks you will get a bank transfer from Amazon into your bank.

The other upside to this is that if you have taken on Amazon's fulfilment service then all your stock is not only being sold through your web store and your marketplace account with your stock management system fully engaged but Amazon are picking it, packing it and sending it for you.

Therefore as a solution to your retail business it could be very valuable indeed and you should spend a little bit of time looking at the option and getting a full understanding of the possibilities of using the option along with any restrictions it may have on using other platforms not supported by Amazon if you wish to continue expand your business.

If you check out Amazon's fee structure you will find that it is very competitive to other shopping carts in the marketplace as you are not paying the Amazon seller fee that would be applicable when selling in the Amazon marketplace. This means if your web store is lucrative and shopped on a regular basis it could be a win-win all round for both you and Amazon.

What You Can Do If You Sell On Other Platforms, EBay, Play.Com Etc.

If you're going to sell across multiple platforms, the idea of this may sound like an awful lot of extra work, your sales are going to grow immensely. The interesting thing is if you start by listing your items from a spreadsheet to each platform then you are always going to have the basic data for each product in one place.

Therefore, it is just as easy to upload an item onto eBay as it is to upload an item onto Amazon and onto your own web store.

Each of the different platforms has its own criteria with its own unique look and feel on how the products can be presented. Once you realise that the information you are putting on to each platform is virtually identical then you will start to see how all you need to do is manipulate the data slightly in specific areas.

- EBay title bar is currently a maximum of 80 characters including spaces.
- Amazon's title bar is currently a maximum of 250 characters.
- Your own website title bar will be different again.

This means that you need to have three titles. But each title will contain similar keywords along with specific descriptive words. So on eBay you have to be very conscious of the amount of space you're using to ensure you get the best keywords in the title bar. With Amazon the current title bar is longer so you have more flexibility and can be slightly more descriptive in your title although you will be using the same keywords and product description. You may find that your Amazon title will fit into your web store title or vice versa.

By keeping the data about the item on a master spreadsheet this means that you can extract the required data for each platform in the correct order. Your product description for all of the platforms will be virtually identical. You will have bullet points on Amazon that you don't have on eBay.

I tend to extract the best information out of the description and turn it into the five bullet points that Amazon require, so I am not creating new information I am merely duplicating some of the information that I've already written for the description in a shorten format.

So you can see that selling across different platforms may take slightly longer to manually upload the product information but let's say you're selling across three platforms then you are getting three for the price of one and a little bit of time and effort on your part.

Success Tip: get into the habit of ensuring all your data is stored on a master spreadsheet, this way if you upgrade or integrate your systems in the future you are going to have all of the information to hand so that you can complete such an integration fairly smoothly. It is always worth beginning with the end in mind.

Stock Control Made Easy With Third-Party Applications

If like me when I started the business I started selling on eBay only then migrated to Amazon, play.com and of course my own web stores. Initially as we were growing the business I was using spreadsheets and manipulating the spreadsheets on a regular basis to ensure the stock was correct.

This meant that physical checks were required by the team that were working for me on the packing side of the business. They were instructed to tell me when, visually, they noticed we were getting low on certain stock lines. This was absolutely fine where lines were repeatable by reordering from the supplier, however, I also bought over the years many end of line products that were not repeatable so we had to devise a system that when we got to the last five of an item we would keep a very close eye on the sales so that they didn't oversell. We oversold on a regular basis purely because we were too busy to focus on the requirements of stock management.

My team now uses a piece of software called Linnworks, we pay a fee every month for the use of the software, but what it allows us to do is to integrate all of our listings across multiple channels. For our business it is great because not only does it manage the stock control, it manages the customer orders, it will manage refunds and returns.

For us it is a very cost-effective way to manage our business across all of our selling platforms and web stores. It also leaves us free to deal with sourcing new products to sell.

The great thing about this software is we only have to load the details of the item once and it then automatically sends that information in the format we require to the sales page. Now obviously each platform has its own little quirks so what we send to eBay will be designed to go to eBay and what we send to Amazon will be written and designed to go to Amazon as I indicated earlier.

There is another benefit to using this type of software as it also can be used as a CRM system (Customer Relationship Management). This means if I want to run a promotion I have access to historical data for my customers purchase history along with contact information so that I can reach them with whatever my new offer may be.

There are a number of applications out there that will offer you stock control management systems. The first one we ever used was a system called 'channelgrabber' which we migrated from after we stopped holding stock ourselves and had all of our stock outsourced to various fulfilment houses, however this piece of software is very cost-effective and is worth looking at the very beginning of your journey if you are needing to use a third party stock control system. I also know that the team at channelgrabber are constantly making enhancements to the software.

Channel Advisor is also another company that will help build a more bespoke platform for you, this does come at a cost, they are a professional company and are worth checking out to get some ideas and quotes from.

If you do a Google search for online retail stock management systems you will find that there are plenty out there to choose from.

Grow Your Business By Selling On Multiple Platforms

The advantage to having multiple platforms is you have a far greater chance of being found in the Internet competitive retail space, when Google for instance is searching the web for the words a potential customer has typed into the search bar, assuming you have used keywords or key phrases that match the customers search term, you are going to have a better chance of having one of your sites coming up on page 1 of Google. Most of the time it will be your eBay or Amazon sites, but occasionally if you've got the keyword strategy absolutely right it may be your web store that comes up alongside Amazon and eBay.

Now I'm not going to get into Googles criteria for algorithms, but briefly Google will constantly search the web for new, relevant and informative data. Therefore if your product has good quality relevant and informative data you have a very good chance of Google adding you to the list of successful searches.

If your data is across multiple platforms then your data will be seen on multiple occasions, but will not be seen as duplicated data because you have it listed across the multiple platforms. If your data is listed in other countries and in other languages again you are increasing the chance of your product being found ahead of your competition.

So by having multiple platforms and ensuring that you keep them updated, making seasonal or special occasion changes to your keywords (i.e. Valentine's Day, Mother's Day, winter, summer etc.) your site is always going to be changing and active therefore Google is always going to be looking at your changes which will help keep you higher in the search rankings.

Higher search rankings, mean more visits and that means more sales.

Setting Your Price Across Multiple Platforms

This is an easy one for me. I like to have price continuity, it's not always easy to achieve but I always start out with that in mind. If I start discounting a product on one site and hold it at a higher price on another site then all this does is devalues my product from the customer's perspective.

Online shoppers are becoming extremely savvy, they will find the item they are looking for and they may go away and search for it again. If you have your item priced on your eBay store at £29.99, amazon at £31.99, play.com £30.99 and your own web store at £28.99 this does not look good to them so they may decide to go elsewhere.

I appreciate that different platforms charge different fees and have different fee structures, however I take the view that I want price continuity across all my selling platforms. Therefore if a customer finds an item I am selling on one platform it will be exactly the same price on the other platform. This helps to build levels of trust with your customers and they will accept your pricing policy rather than asking you why are you selling at different prices across different platforms.

In the next chapter I will show you my simple cost calculator that will help you decide on your selling price.

When I am analysing other people's selling platforms this is an area that I come across on a regular basis, I know that you think you're just passing on the fees and costs to the customer, but you are making yourself look as if you were an unprofessional seller. Far better to have a good price continuity across all of your platforms rather than look unprofessional.

The one area where you can make differences on price is on international sales where you are converting to other currencies. You will need to add a small margin for currency fluctuation as your price in that currency will stay fixed regardless of the exchange rate. And of course as the exchange rate varies your price will stay fixed you need to remain protected. So you may need to implement a slightly different strategy for international pricing in other currencies.

However, if you're selling on several international platforms the same rules apply to ensure that the product is shown at the same price across your international platforms.

Chapter 4 How To Find Niche Products That Sell With A Profit

Do Your Research In Advance

As stated earlier in the book, I will always do a great deal of research into a product before I actually purchase it. I get approached by company representatives and importers on a regular basis, they have all got one aim in mind, to sell me something. When they come in with their products I have a number of questions that I ask them quite bluntly and upfront. I would urge you to ask similar questions.

- Which multiple retailers currently stock the product?
    - If this product is being stocked by a large multiple retail chain or supermarket I will be looking to see how they sell the product, and at what point they discount the sales price of the product. It may be that they only have the product at a particular time of year, Christmas, Mother's Day, summer, etc. Therefore this may not eliminate the product as a line I would be happy to stock although they would have it for a peak period, I could stock it throughout the year assuming that there was a good potential for year-round sales but the big multiple retailers could not afford to hold the stock all year round.

- Do you have a direct supply arrangement with Amazon?
    - If they are supplying Amazon direct, then the chances are I am not even going to take the conversation any further, Amazon negotiate very good deals with suppliers and you will very often find that they will discount the product quite heavily or offer free shipping opportunities at a level that you cannot compete. My personal rule of thumb is that if Amazon are buying it directly I'm not stocking it.
- Which other online retailers do you supply?
    - I will then want to look at the retailers they are supplying, have a look at their list price, discounted price and sales price. I may have to look at historical product data that does not apply to the particular product itself. However, I need to understand how my competition works so that I do not purchase a product that is going to be unprofitable.
- If I buy your product to sell online will I get exclusivity?
    - This question quite often will throw a sales representative into a little bit of a quandary, they know that they cannot stop other retailers selling online, that is not the purpose of my question what I am looking for is exclusivity to be the only online retailer that can sell the product.
    - Now there may be some terms and conditions that you have to negotiate, however if you can get exclusivity, that means you can control the

pricing policy of the product a lot more than if it was in the general market place. The advantage to the selling company is quite simple. If there is no price erosion then margins can remain healthy, this is good for both the company off-line retailers and ourselves as online retailers.
  - By obtaining exclusivity in the online sector and delivering excellent sales results you can build excellent relationships with that particular supplier and become the online retailer of choice for any new products they may add to their portfolio.
- Do you import direct from the manufacturer or are you an agent?
  - You need to understand how many people are taking a percentage of the profit, if the company is an agent for an importer who is purchasing from an agent say in China who is acting for the manufacturer who is also based in China there are four people in the supply chain all wanting to take some profit.
  - Therefore, you need to be as close to the beginning of the supply chain as possible, I am not suggesting you enter into an import agreement, however I am suggesting that you cut out as many of the middlemen taking profit as possible so that you can have the best purchase price which means that you can have the best

margin for the product when you are selling it online.
- What is my minimum order quantity?
    - You may be pleasantly surprised, I come across minimum order quantities of as little as one unit and as many as 300 units. You need to ask the question to understand how you are going to hold stock against predicted sales volume.
- What is the inbound supply chain and how regularly do you replenish your stock?
    - There are a number of wholesalers and importers who will always have backup stock available in holding warehouses within the UK. However, there are a number of smaller operators that cannot afford to do this and will only order stock on a needs must basis. If you have a supplier who works on a needs must basis you will have issues with continuity of supply especially if you have taken the time and trouble to list the items in such a way that you are getting good sales volume.
- What level of discounts are available?
    - One of two things will happen when you ask this question, the representative will panic or they will give you a straight and an immediate answer with their pricing policy and their terms. If they go into a panic then you've got some room to negotiate on whatever price they initially come back with. If they go straight into an immediate

answer with all of the information you need to write that down and then ask them to come back to you with some better terms. The chances are that they will do so as there is normally further movement but it may need higher authority sign off.
- What quantity do I need to order to get the best discount?
    - This comes down to negotiating skills, they may wish you to take 1000 units which may be too much for you, but if your research shows that you can sell three items a day on average then you may be able to give them a promissory order for 1000 units spread out over a one-year period.
    - I have found many companies in the UK that are quite happy to take advanced orders on the basis that you promised to take the stock over a period of time at that discounted rate. This is a great negotiating strategy.

You now have a great deal of information about the product, about pricing and about the competition. So before you make your final decision you need to do your research.

Sometimes I do this with a company representative present so that they can see exactly what I'm looking for, this will do two things for me, one is it will show the representative exactly how we target our market, it will also give them an insight into how they need to find products suitable for us so that they do not waste time with products that are not profitable

The first thing to do is check out your competition for the other retailers that purchase the products and then look at their historical data to see how they sell or discount products throughout the sales cycle.

As an example you will find towards Christmas, large toy sellers will discount lines very early by up to 30% off the recommended retail selling price, if the lines do not move quickly enough they may discount heavily in order that they are not left holding stock. If you are selling the same or similar products you need to understand this strategy and ensure that if they discount at heavy margins you can compete without losing money.

Next is to do a Google search and see what prices people are asking for the product by doing some price comparisons and you also need to include shipping in these price comparisons as some retailers will offer free post, therefore you need to add the cost of the postage into your selling price.

Then you're straight onto Amazon, eBay, play.com and any of the other platforms that the product is sold so that you can see the existing price, the sales history and have a look at that competitor to see how good they are at listing the products, how good their descriptions are and whether they are a real threat to you I very often find that a number of these companies are not a direct threat because they have very poor listings.

Analyse The Potential Net Profit Net Of A Product Before You Buy Stock

Question: if I purchase an item for £10 and sell it for £30 free post what is my net profit?

When I am doing my seminars I ask this question, the answer I get ranges from £20 down to £14. At the time of writing this book nobody has ever given me a close answer to the truth.

Here is a quick example:

Stock cost	£10.00	the physical cost per item from my supplier
Selling Price	£30.00	the average price I would expect to obtain for each item that I sell, on that basis I may buy 100 items, sell 10 at full suggested retail price, 60 items at my desired price, 20 items at a clearance price, 10 items left in

		stock to cover losses damages returns and failed deliveries.
Packer Time	£0.60	this will depend on how you will fulfil your orders, but in my case this is roughly the cost we would pay for each item being picked ready for dispatch
Packaging	£0.80	the added cost of packaging which may be a small grey bag or it could be a large box, you need to factor in all or any packaging materials.
Seller Fees	£5.16	I work on an average cost of 17.2% in seller fees, this is a good indicator and is roughly about the figure you will be charged by Amazon, you also have to take into account that you will have a final value seller fee from eBay, as well as a listing fee, and if they're paying by PayPal you will have to pay a PayPal fee. If you are using Google shopping on your web store you may be paying per click, therefore this figure is a good benchmark.

VAT-Net Payable	£3.00	in the UK the VAT rate is currently 20% when I purchased my item I can claim the VAT back when I sell the item to my customer I then have to pay the VAT to HMRC, so this figure is the differential between the amount I claim back and the amount I charge the customer
Free p&p	£4.80	customers love free postage and packing, but you have to add it into your overall selling price as DHL or Royal Mail do not deliver anything free.
Returns 2%	£0.60	I also use the figure of 2% of the gross value of sales price to put a figure against the cost of returns, damages, non-deliveries or refunds. Our present rate is less than 2% of our sales therefore this gives me a margin per item that I can allocate towards those refunds and losses.
Gross Profit	£5.04	in my calculation this represents the amount of potential gross profit

		after the deduction of the cost listed against the purchase price.
Gross Margin	**50.40%**	my calculation this represents the percentage of potential gross profit after the deduction of the cost listed against the purchase price

In this quick example you will see that I am left with a potential gross profit of £5.04, this does not take into account my operational costs: rent, wages, telephone, consumables, local taxes. Therefore if I was to add that cost my net return could be as low as £2.60.

I use this as a spreadsheet as an initial guide when I'm looking at new product opportunities, if I have a company representative with me at the time then they are able to see how I'm working things out which helps them find products that I may be interested in that will work for me.

Trade Events And Trade Shows

Trade events are a great way to pick up ideas, contacts and opportunities. There are numerous trade events throughout the year and most are held every year at about the same time. Importers spend many thousands of pounds on the trade stand, it is their time to showcase their goods, mix with their existing customer base, find new customers and also to see what their competition are doing.

The big international trade fairs are held in China, Germany, United Kingdom as well as other locations throughout the world, it is easy to find them, just type into Google international trade shows for the country that you desire. I spend around 18 to 20 days per annum visiting different trade events. I have one rule that I will never break at a trade event and that is 'I never place a confirmed order at the event'.

You have to remember that these companies spend thousands of pounds to showcase their products, they are looking for a return on their investment and that return is confirmed orders from prospective buyers. Now although I will ask all of the same questions outlined earlier at the trade event, some agents may not be quite as truthful in their answers.

You must always come away from the trade event with the information and do your research, it is always good to speak to the company after the event and ask them a few more questions about how well the event went on how well their products were received along with the other questions about who has purchased and who will be selling online.

At these events you also want to be asking about their pricing policy, you need to know what their suggested retail prices and then you need to know what their internal terms and conditions are in continued supply of goods to people who may heavily discount the products. Now there is a trading law which means you cannot fix pricing, however if they are selling to hundreds of retailers and each retailer is discounting to beat the other on price, the product will eventually just be seen as a cheap line in the market place and the product will become devalued. You do not want these type of products, you want ones where there is an understanding that nobody wants to price cut and that margins require to be held at good levels. This means you are all trying to sell at similar prices and it becomes a matter of how good you are at getting your product in front of the customer with your marketing and keyword strategies.

Buying Stock By Tender, Public, And Trade Auctions

Over the years I have done really well with this type of purchase, a couple of examples below.

Pizza Paddle Case Study:

I managed to source these items through one of my secret contacts, I bought a job lot of 760 which we sold through eBay, Amazon and one of our websites.

They were sold all around the world. The recommended retail price at the time was £19.99. I purchased them for £1.62 each (£1,231.20)

They were sold on a special offer at £11.99 each plus postage and packing, my net return after eBay Amazon and PayPal fees was in excess of £6600.

Wax Muffin/Cupcake Case Study:

Looking at something nobody else wanted to purchase! A pallet of cupcake cases. 36 boxes x 24 sleeves per box x 100 cupcake cases per sleeve. Purchased for £5.

These were not your cheap and cheerful paper muffin cases, these were for professional kitchens they were pleated and they were waxed. Our biggest market for selling these was USA and Australia! We were selling them for £4.99 per sleeve plus postage and packing.

After fees and costs we made in excess of £2800 net profit from a £5 purchase.

You will be given the information on the training workshop where you can to find these opportunities. Just one such opportunity will more than double your investment.

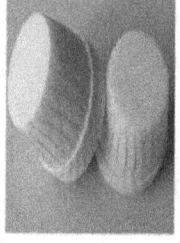

There are always going to be opportunities for you to find a product and turn it into good cash returns. The key to this is being observant, if you are purchasing in auction and a lot of people are excited about a particular piece of stock than possibly the price is going to be too high so you may have to look at things that people are not so excited about. As in the two examples above.

When purchasing in auction please remember that you will also have to pay an auctioneers fee, so you need to add the fee to the price then add transportation costs if there are any (van hire, Courier collection, travel to the auction to inspect the goods etc). I have come across a number of people who have purchased what they thought was a bargain in auction only to find out that the true market value is almost the cost price that they have paid because they got so excited. To purchase in auction you need to be fairly calm and keep a clear business head-on and know when to pull out of the bidding.

With auction purchases you always had chance to view the catalogue which means that you always have a chance to research online the products you're looking at so that you have the best possible chance of purchasing and a price that is good for you with an opportunity to sell at a price that makes you money.

Purchasing by tender is a slightly different way of competing for stock, the interesting thing about purchasing by tender is that you have less competition, most people do not want the hassle of having to go and examined the stock, and then put a formal bid together in which to make the purchase. Therefore tenders are brilliant ways in which you can purchase line is extremely cheaply.

Purchasing by tender is normally price driven, so the person offering the most money for the items in theory should win the tender. However, I work on the basis of offering additional information to the tender, it may be that funds will be transferred immediately upon being awarded the tender, it may be that I will add comments such as, we will arrange for collection of the goods within 48 hours of our tender being accepted, we may put in there that we will clear away all of the non-saleable items to dispose of at our own cost to leave the site, free and clear.

The reason that you will put different things in is to make your tender look better than just on price, so the company handling the tender has less work to do and you are giving them a better benefit, it may be that you take all the non-saleable stuff which leaves them with an empty unit that they can then advertise on lease without having to do a major clean-up.

Success Tip: by offering them some additional benefits to your tender being accepted, you will also then be looked upon favourably for future opportunities, and when you take away the non-saleable items you will always find that you can put them onto eBay or Gumtree at a small cost and somebody will normally come along and make a purchase. It may not be much but it goes towards your costs.

Easy Ways To Find Liquidated And Bankrupt Stock

Finding opportunities in auctions is simple, you just need to know where to look, many of the online auctions are easy to bid on from the comfort of your home/office. There are also many trade only auctions held throughout the UK we can either make sealed bids, telephone bids or obviously attend the auction in person.

The two companies I've listed below host many online auctions on behalf of auctioneers:

- www.i-bidder.co.uk and they also have a .com site.
- www.bidspotter.co.uk and also they have a .com site.

These two great places to start your research and you will find that auctions are listed to several weeks in advance so that you can study the items carefully and create a plan of how you are going to bid on each particular listing.

In the UK you can also subscribe to a weekly publication both online and also receive a weekly catalogue of forthcoming auctions in the post. I have subscribed to this for many years and have made some really good purchases from spotting opportunities.

- www.auctionnews.co.uk

This particular company also produces the Golden Nugget (in my opinion) of information that if you are fully focused and prepared to do a little bit of extra legwork you can actually make purchases of items before they even get moved to auction rooms or put into tender processes.

They produce a magazine which shows all of the company insolvencies that have been registered on a weekly basis. This is public record information that will come through the courts from winding up petitions or liquidations and other information obtained from Companies House.

The information that you will obtain is the name of the company, the name of the appointed administrator and the contact details for the administrator.

This is where your legwork comes in, you do a Google search on the company to find out what business they were involved with, this is going to give you an idea of whether it was just a shell company that had no assets, or it was a trading company would have had resalable and tangible assets, or if it was a company that may have held physical stock for the retail sector.

Once you have identified a company where you think there may be some saleable and tangible assets or stock what you then do is prepare a formal letter to send to the administrator (see sample below). This letter doesn't need to be very long it is purely introducing yourself as a potential interested third party in acquiring the stock or assets of the company if they were prepared to allow you to make a formal offer. In this letter you will ask them for a quick reply and if they have any schedule showing the assets and/or stock that may be available.

Your first objective is to get that letter over to the administrator, go to the administrator's company website obtain a relevant email address, fax number, physical address and telephone number.

Now that you have these details you need to email and fax the letter over, make a telephone call to confirm they have received your communication. At this point you will then sit back and wait for approximately 48 hours for them to make contact with you, if you have not heard from them within 48 hours then make a telephone call asked to speak to the administrator so that you can obtain their position and start any negotiation.

This is a very powerful way in which you can find stock and make serious money, the job of an administrator is to wind up the affairs of the company in the most cost efficient way by disposing of any stock and assets for the best potential price in the marketplace. The benefit of you approaching them direct and making them an offer is that this reduces the time, effort and money involved in advertising, sending to auction or marketing the stock and assets. So you are in a very advantageous position to negotiate an extremely good deal.

[Date]

[Type the sender company name]

[Type the sender company address]

[Type the recipient name]

[Type the recipient address]

[Type the salutation]

[Ref; company XYZ Limited in Liquidation]

I am writing to you to express an interest in the above named company as you are the appointed administrator of the company's affairs.

I am currently looking to acquire certain assets and/or stock that you may be looking to dispose of in dealing with the liquidation.

I would therefore, request that you will forward me any details you have regarding the assets and/or stock so that I can make you a very speedy and fair offer to purchase immediately.

I look forward to receiving your reply.

[Type the closing]

Andrew

[Type the sender title]

Create Your Own Branded Bespoke Labelled Products

Once you have got established and you find products that sell very well for you, you may want to look at differentiating the product from that of your competition, the easiest way to do this is to talk to your supplier about creating your own branded products, also known as own label products.

A major advantage of going down this route is that you create an item that is exclusively yours and not available to any other third party. By creating your own brand or label you may be able to negotiate better purchasing prices as you will have to agree to purchase minimum order quantities.

You will also be changing the product in some way to avoid any copyright or trademark issues unless you already have an agreement with that particular copyright or trademark owner. Now you are building an edge in the marketplace which means you will obtain greater profits, negotiated lower purchase costs, although you may have higher storage costs to take into consideration.

This has worked very successfully for our business in which we created a number of niche markets where we have brought our own label product that gives us exclusivity in that marketplace and is led us to achieve greater profits. A word of caution, you need to be absolutely 100% sure that you have a product that will sell before confirm the transaction. You need to be extremely aware of your competition.

You have a number of options in the way you do this, you can either find a manufacturer or import directly yourself, Ali Baba is a great place to start looking for good manufacturing contacts. Or, as I tend to favour personally, you can go to your existing supply chain and negotiate a deal that works for both of you. The benefit of using your existing supply chain is firstly they do not lose your business, and secondly they are taking the risk and dealing with all the paperwork of the shipping and importation documentation for you and if there was a problem, you will be able to reject them and it will become their problem to deal with the manufacturer.

Handmade Crafted And Unique Products

Many online sellers start out from turning their hobby into a business, this takes a lot of dedicated focus as sometimes the great hobby that you had can turn out to be a total nightmare of the business as it grows above and beyond your control. Basically there are not enough hours in the day for you to continue your hobby, run the business and lead the lifestyle that you desire.

If you are going to go down this route create benchmarks for yourself, if the product that you produce has a high ticket value and requires low-volume manufacture or requires to be totally handmade with your signature (as in a piece of artwork) then you need to price your work appropriately with high returns and keep your business small but highly profitable.

Using the various platforms that we have spoken about this gives you an ideal opportunity to market your products and gain recognition in your particular niche. You may decide not to use some of the more popular platforms and take your product to some of the smaller more bespoke platforms such as 'Not On The High Street' for example.

The reverse of that is if you have created a unique product, you can then look at having all or part of its components produced in greater quantities, you will need to decide whether you want to have it mass produced in for arguments sake say China at a really low cost, or whether you would want to brand it is 'Made In Britain' so that you can leverage its value to discerning customers that like to purchase unique items that are 'Made In Britain'. This has a great international sales appeal. And if your product is photographed, marketed and in some cases even videoed you will be able to obtain a premium price for your premium product.

How To Find End Of Line And Clearance Products

When I first started selling online a number of years ago end of line and clearance products were extremely cheap. I was able to pick up end of line products from the large multiple retailers through various brokers at between 7% and 10% of the recommended retail price.

As more and more people have decided to start selling online, car boot sales, garage sales, these brokers have recognised that there is a bigger market here and we're now seeing prices as high as 15 to 25% of the recommended retail price that they were previously on display at.

Therefore, when you are purchasing these products from these brokers you need to have a good look at the marketplace to see what the price has levelled to. If these items had cleared through at 50% of the recommended retail price then that is probably where you have got to position and sell those products going forward. So you've got to be able to make sure using the calculator shown earlier in the book that the item you are selling still commands a profitable return.

I come across many people who purchase these products and do not do their research first, and they find they are left with items that are potentially saturated in the marketplace and the price is being constantly driven down and they are only making 30 to 40% of the recommended retail price.

So there is your warning, research your products before you purchase them, however, there are many brokers out there that trade in various other items. They very often sell them by the pallet, so you are able to go and purchase at fairly low cost a pallet that may be all one product or a mixed lot so that you can start trading them online. A lot of part-time online sellers will go for the branded product before they go for the non-branded product as they have the perception that they will get more money for the branded goods.

There is money to be made in all of the sectors, and a great place to start is with a UK publication called The Trader, this magazine is available in most large newsagents, and also has a website version. This magazine will give you many of the UK wholesalers and brokers trading in stock and you will be able to visit their websites to see the various lots they have available with a good indication of purchase price.

Sourcing Pre-Owned Or Graded Returned Products

This is an area where you can make very high gains, you will need to have good storage facilities and you will also need to be confident in your abilities to dismantle parts, refurbish items that may be damaged or broken, have the time to test items before you sell them.

Dealing in graded/returned products is more time-consuming. When you purchase a pallet or container of pre-owned or graded items you will very rarely have any indication for the reason that they have been returned. Some companies do grade their products so you may get some clue from that grading, unwanted item, opens not used, damaged, faulty, warranty return and there could be many more.

If you are purchasing returns that have been graded as not wanted or not faulty, you will still need to take them out of the original packaging check that all of the component parts are there and that the item works and that it is not damaged or faulty.

When you are advertising this type of item it is highly recommended that you take photographs of the item as it is showing any blemishes, marks or damage so that the customer cannot come back to you and say that your description was incorrect.

When you are advertising a product with a fault, put as much of the detail about the fault as possible, you will be surprised how much people will pay to purchase faulty items if they have the capability to rectify the fault. This is a very lucrative market as you will be purchasing the items at hugely discounted prices.

Another favourite for a lot of online sellers is to break items down into their component parts. These parts have a value and can be sold extremely well by using model and part numbers in your keywords when you advertise online. Your customer base for parts can be other business owners who run repair shops or the person who already has the item in their home and is confident enough to create their own effective repair.

How To Bundle Products To Reduce Competition

A number of the Internet retailers and I speak to who are selling mass-market products with a lot of competition continue to 'Sail In The Sea Of Sameness' and do not look at other ways of differentiating their offering.

When you are selling on Amazon you have the opportunity to sell your product in the same listing somebody else who already sells a product. The majority of retailers go down that route and they will reduce their price below that of the other seller so that they can be the cheapest in order to get the highly prized 'buy button'.

This then leads to price erosion, as your competitor notices their sales drop or that are price changes happening on their Amazon dashboard, they will then go and lower their price below yours, you then do the same, your competitor does the same and all you end up doing is devaluing the product and losing any chance of making a good profit.

So you need to differentiate your offering to that of the competition, one way of doing this is to bundle products, let us say that you have a miniature blue campervan clock, of which there are some 20 other sellers selling the same product. You may also have a miniature campervan key ring.

Why not bundle these together to create a new listing, you now have a miniature blue campervan clock and key ring gift set. Now you can do this with almost anything, and it doesn't just have to be two items you can make up gift sets in any proportion. It is down to your imagination and also to a little bit of research to find out what people are buying.

This way you can leave your competitors to battle out the price war, but you will have a completely different offering to your potential customers which will give you the opportunity to increase your profitability. You can always then add little extras such as gift wrap and gift messaging services.

On the basis you market this correctly you are giving your customer added value, the perception of a superior offering to that of the competition.

Chapter 5 The Secrets To Great Listings That Are Easily Found

How To Write A Great Product Description

Your description of your product is not the first thing that people see in making their mind up about whether to purchase your product. Selling on the internet is about the visual as well as about the written word. Therefore, before you write your description you need to make sure that you have got great photographs (more on photography below).

If you have a poor description or no description, something I see quite often, you have not got a very good chance of selling your product. Because you are not giving the customer the opportunity to find out about the product and understand all the details of the product. When you write a good description you are also giving the customer your sales pitch.

Consider the customer in a little more detail, they have found your item they have clicked through to your description on the sales page and you have given them the specification of the product. What you may not have done, and I see this regularly, is given them a reason to buy your product. This is your opportunity to close the sale in a written format.

So your description is very powerful, and needs to be treated as your sales pitch and method of closing the sale. You do not want them to click away onto somebody else's page you want them to stay on your page and click on the buy button. customers a very good at following instructions, so you need to instruct them in the description to go and place the product to their shopping basket or click the buy now button. If you tell them to do this you have a greater chance of them actually doing so.

So below are a few key points to remember when writing great descriptions:

- tell them positively how good the product this
- tell them the features along with the benefits of buying your product
- give them easy options to buy, free post, gift wrap etc.
- tell them to make the purchase 'Add To Basket'
- if your product has features against other competing products tell them benefits of those features

Give Accurate Product Dimensions

Giving customers accurate dimensions of both the product and the packaging, is a really top-quality idea. First of all it reduces the inbound emails to you by them asking you "what are the dimensions?". Where possible it is always useful to list the dimensions in both imperial and metric measurements, as this satisfies both markets and you are leaving less for your potential customer to have to do for themselves, which means they are less likely to click away from your page

Some things I see very often is that people will put the dimensions in small font or near the end of the description, I would suggest that you put the dimensions in the most appropriate place in the description and also make sure that they are clearly visible and not hidden.

Putting the dimensions of the packaging within Amazon is fairly straightforward, the spreadsheet templates, and the listing tool has those boxes already set up. By giving the customer the dimensions and of course the weight of the item will help them in their buying decision.

A product that we have sold quite regularly in the past is a concrete garden bench, it weighs approximately 25 kg boxed. Part of our target demographic for this product are elderly and retired customers. Therefore, because they have been given the weight of the item when it has been delivered they have been able to make arrangements with friends, family or neighbours to assist them to assemble the bench. On this basis they are also able to ask friends, family or neighbours if they will be prepared to assist them before they can make the final buying decision.

How To Use Amazon Bullet Points

Amazon will give you five lines of up to 250 characters per line to use as bullet points, these bullet points normally appear next to the photographs on the sales page. So what tends to happen is the photograph will appear on the left-hand side of the screen, the title will appear at the top of the screen and the bullet points are very prominently placed in this centre of the screen.

This positioning draws the eyes towards the descriptive words and being as they are set in such a way by only having up to 250 characters per line they are easy to read and help make the buying decision a lot easier.

My personal formula for this is as follows:

1. the first bullet point is softened version of my keyword rich title
2. This line is the most important details out of the description
3. This line I use to put the second most important details out of the description
4. This line is where I put relevant dimensions and measurements
5. Here I would put benefits of making the purchase or closing the sale

As you can see by using this formula I am getting over the key points of the product to the client, I am giving them some of the benefits of making the purchase, and I am closing the sale or given them the reason to purchase from the now.

How To Use Brilliant Photography

A great photograph should be very clear and crisp, have a plain white background, you need to make some small lighting adjustments to remove shadows, if you are using a material backdrop then you need to make sure there are no creases in the material. And take a number of shots at different angles. You have then got the opportunity to find the best shots of that particular product. Where possible I would avoid using the supplier's stock photographs other than as secondary photographs rather than primary photographs.

Do not put borders around the photograph, do not put text into the photographs as the platforms that you're selling on do not like it and could remove your product from sale altogether, now if Amazon removes a product you will not know about it until such time as you notice it is no longer there.

This is not a book about product photography, so what has the photography got to do with your description. The answer that is quite simple they see your photograph before they see your description, so they are going to click through onto the sales page from the photograph of your product and/or the detail in the title (which I will be covering in the next chapter)

Success tip: when you take your photographs your camera will automatically upload them to your computer normally with a numerical reference that is generated by the camera that you are using. What most people do is continue to use that numerical reference. I want you to do something slightly different I want you to use keywords to retitle that photograph. A photograph that is uploaded with keywords is searchable by the search engines. So your keyword strategy also applies to your photography.

Offer Fast And Free Delivery Options

Everybody likes free delivery, you and I in the real world know there is no such thing as free delivery! The cost of the delivery has got to be added into the price of your product, it is coming out of the gross profit you are making on that product.

If you are selling volume related products that are price sensitive then you will probably offer the basic standard delivery which will be your cheapest option and you will add that into your price. From there you can then offer them an upgrade within the Amazon structure. In Amazon structure and upgrade will move the postage service from standard to expedited. Amazon don't define what expedited means but the customers will be given an anticipated delivery date from the information you will put into the settings for your postage services when you open your Amazon account.

If your standard settings are 3 to 5 days then the customer will be anticipating the item delivery within that period of time and Amazon will advise them of that at the point of purchase automatically.

If your expedited delivery is 1 to 2 days then again Amazon will advise the customer of that accordingly at the point of purchase. In my business I treat expedited as being required the next working day, so we price expedited delivery based on next day delivery rates.

You can set your pricing for the next day delivery as required, you may also want to add a little bit of margin to that price as this customer is jumping ahead of the queue. You will have obviously worked out the price of the item and will set it in the shipping details accordingly, plus a small margin.

Although you can set your default shipping within the settings of Amazon, you can also do shipping overrides, which means every item that you have can have its own shipping price appended to it. This is done through downloading a spreadsheet template from Amazon putting in the SKU codes of the products you want to change the shipping price to and then you are able to enter in shipping prices for that product for the UK, UK expedited, Europe and that is split up into European regions so you can vary the price and also worldwide shipping.

If your products are held by Amazon in their fulfilment centre and the customer is a 'Prime Customer' they are automatically going to be guaranteed expedited delivery from Amazon. And of course you can amend the shipping price for expedited and European or worldwide delivery as mentioned above.

Always offer your customers the choice of expedited delivery, even if you personally believe that it is expensive, it is up to the customer to decide whether it is expensive not you, the customer may have a particular need of that item quickly so the cost of postage becomes irrelevant.

We have a particular line of products that sell for £3.50 in the UK, for a customer to have them expedited to nextday UK delivery the charge is £4.99. We sell hundreds of these items every week, and every week we have lots of people that pay the additional expedited fee to get the item next day. So they are paying more for the postage and the after the item.

Ask Customers For Reviews Of Your Product

Once you have sold your item, and the customer has received it you may wish to ask that customer for a review of the product. More reviews you get on a product the higher that product will be profiled within the Amazon search criteria. Amazon likes products with good reviews, Google and the other search engines also like good reviews.

You should obtain as many reviews as possible and continuously obtain reviews on products even where you may already have a number of reviews. It can only give you more visibility within the search criteria.

The way to get reviews are quite simple, you ask for them.

- Send a thank you note or email several days after delivery of the product and ask for a review.
- Offer a discount on their next purchase if they leave you a review (you do not want to do this from the point of view of bribery, you do want good and bad reviews, the reward of a discount on their next purchase is to thank them for taking the time and trouble to post the review online).
- You may offer to send them a free gift once a review has been posted, same principle applies as above.

- Do not try to get fake reviews, you need genuine reviews from genuine customers who have purchased your product.

Reviews are becoming more and more important to the customer shopping habits, you only have to look at the success of Trip Advisor, before you book a hotel or a holiday online most people will go and look at the reviews on Trip Advisor and that helps them formulate their buying decision. So you need to switch on to getting product reviews and you need to put a plan in place to make sure that you regularly asking customers to leave you a review.

If the review is bad then you need to deal with the negative points in the review as far as that customer is concerned and ask them to amend the review to reflect your good customer service assuming that there review is an honest review of your product. If the review is in any way offensive or is not dealing with the product, you can always make contact with the customer service team who may be able to remove the review from the site.

Chapter 6 Great Titles That Sell More Of Your Products

Why Is The Title So Important?

What is a title, it is a set of primary keywords that are used by search engines to match the data the potential customer has typed into the search box with the product you are trying to sell.

I see so many titles that have virtually no keywords, that to me is unbelievable. Consider for a minute you are the customer looking to make a purchase of a camera. Now if you just put the word camera into Google you are going to get millions of search hits as it is too broad. So if in your listing you only put in the title as a word camera you are not going to be easily found.

Let's say you put in the wording Canon camera, now you may have a slightly better chance of being found, however you still haven't put in enough detail!

Now let us suggest that you would put in Canon camera DSLR 6100, now you are giving an exact match to a model of a camera so you are bringing yourself up in the search rankings, so these would be primary keywords used as a string at the beginning of your title bar.

You have got to find other keywords which may be secondary keywords that would also help your product to be found. Secondary keywords could be 'photo image stabilising photography zoom lens video technology fast shutter speed' etc.

You will notice that I have not used words like 'and the look cheap best bargain sale price brand-new' to name but a few.

Your title is so important it needs to be highly keyword rich, the wording that you have got to put into your title needs to be relevant to the product, and it needs to be words that somebody will sit in front of their computer and physically type. You need to get your mindset into a position where you look at your keywords differently. Your keywords need to reflect the words that somebody into the search bar to find the product they are looking for.

If somebody wants a Canon camera DSLR 6100 there is a good chance that they are going to type that in as a keyword string, so you have got a good chance of your product being found. They may also decide to type in a broader search looking for Canon camera video, those may be the features that they want so you now have got three of those keywords in your title.

Hopefully you can follow the logic of using good quality and accurate well researched keywords that will work so that you can leave out the words that are wasted. Consider every character that you have in your title bar as currency, that currency may be the difference between financial freedom and no income.

Have A Keyword Strategy That Works

Where do you find keywords, there are lots of places you can look, one of the first things to do is to type the product title into Google and see what comes up on page 1. Then you want to have a look at the organic search results. These are the ones that have got to the page 1 of Google without using one of Google's marketing strategies or paid advertising. You can always tell which ones these paid adverts are as they are normally set within a shaded background. Organic searches normally appear on a plain white background.

The listing that is on page 1 of Google and has got there organically will have some clues, so the first thing you need to do is click into that link and have a look at their title, have a look at the wording that they may have used in the initial description, on header tabs, and if possible on photographs.

This will give you some clues into some keywords you may not have thought about. Then go onto Amazon, when you search for the item in Amazon's search bar it will also prompt you with other options in a box just below the search bar when the result comes up. Again these are clues to keywords that are available.

Google have their own keyword tool, which is designed for people who wish to use Google trends or Google adword campaigns, the tools within Google are free to use, they only become chargeable if you decide to use the information on a particular campaign. By doing your research you will be able to find good quality keywords that you can use as primary keywords for the product title and also as secondary keywords in your product descriptions.

How To Find Short And Long Tail Keywords

Going back to looking at the word camera, that is a short keyword, it is one word and if you put that into Google it would have millions of results, years ago people used to search online in single or double words (short tail keywords).

Today however people tend to search with more words or in short sentences (long tail keywords) so when you are doing your keyword analysis using Google you want to see if there are any long tail keywords searched regularly within the country that you are targeting your product, if there are good-quality long tail keywords and they are searched regularly enough to make a difference then I suggest you look at using those long tail keywords in your titles where possible and your description.

There are some other tools on the market to help you, this is where things may become chargeable. Personally I use some software called Market Samurai, this allows me to put in a keyword and it will generate for me additional keywords and keyword strings (long tail keywords), I can then analyse those keyword strings in greater detail as this software allows me to drill down using laser focused keyword analysis so that I can target my marketing directly to good-quality long tail keywords.

You do need to pay for this type of technology, and there are others available, however this gives me the opportunity to maximise my marketing message and have my products sales pages found online at a higher ranking than would normally be the case.

Success tip: Amazon allows you to put in hidden keywords to which product that you list. If you are listing things manually then you will find it in the listing tab when you go in and edit or list an item. If you are listing from a spreadsheet template then you will find the five columns within the template to take your keywords.

1.	Each line allows you a maximum of 50 characters including spaces
2.	You should put a space after each word or comma for a string of words to make a phrase
3.	You can enter your competitors details here as it is hidden
4.	If you are selling Canon products, you can put the most popular Sony product details here
5.	Use these five lines with fully focused keyword strategies

This is a great feature, and there are so many online retailers selling on Amazon do not use this feature or even know it exists. During a telephone review for somebody who was selling products on Amazon they later claimed there turnover had gone up significantly. Simply by just finding out that they could list keywords against each product that they sell.

To them this and the title keyword strategy was the biggest tip that they picked up from the short telephone call they had with me.

Chapter 7 How To Use The Seasonality Checklist

Some Positive Effects Changing The Keywords In Your Titles Can Have

Now that you have a brief understanding for the necessity of obtaining good keywords you now need the rest of the action planning, if you are selling products for Mother's Day you need to have Mother's Day in your title and as part of your hidden keywords at least eight weeks before Mother's Day. This is because Google will take a little while to start ranking your page, for the new keywords and the other positive affect the changing your keywords to a particular event is you have actually made a change in your product title, description and hidden keywords which is another positive when the search engines are looking for changes and updates.

Therefore if you have a product that you would normally sell all year round and you do not make any changes to the keywords, titles or descriptions then Google may start to reduce your position within the searches due to inactivity. So look for reasons to change your listings, may be look at seasonality or annual event dates and make those changes to have a major positive impact on your online business.

The Best Way To Manage The Seasonal Fluctuations

This sounds easy although it does take time. Time which you should spend wisely on planning ahead for the seasons. The best way to manage the fluctuations and maintain positive cash flow throughout the year is to develop a detailed sales and inventory plan from historic sales before the season begins.

Use this plan to guide the purchase of your inventory to help benchmark when you need to take product from your suppliers, how long it will sit on your shelf, which weeks of the key weeks for selling that product. Halloween, this is a very short selling spike in the annual calendar. It comes around every year without fail in most Western countries. Order your stock early, start marketing it from analysing data to ascertain when the trend for online searches starts, Plan to sell out unless you want to keep the stock until next year. What is the latest cut-off time you can sell it to have it delivered to your customer.

Planning takes time you may think you do not have, but invariably if you take the time to plan carefully your sales will be greater and far more profitable than those that don't.

Before you begin the planning process look at what you sold in the past. If you are a new business and this is your first selling season, talk to trusted supplier representatives, research the Internet trends by using Google analytical tools, look at competitor's websites and study their marketing campaigns. During this planning process you not only need to look at the historical events, you may need to consider the weather conditions for previous year's sales, were the other national or world events that had an impact positively or otherwise, exclude any special orders or special promotional deals you may have had which were one-off opportunities.

You also need to look at the sales cycle: use the assumption you purchase 100 units to sell online and there is a four week period in which online activity trends at a peak (i.e. Halloween). If week one is your launch and you sell 10 units; week two is the peak purchasing period you sell 60 units; week three is the last minute purchases and you sell 20 units with 5 units being purchased after the event for no particular reason - you will have sold a total of 95 units.

Therefore you need to allow for the cost of the remaining 5 units. Also you will need to work on the basis that you are going to have some refunds due to non-delivery, breakage, returns under the rules and regulations adopted by the selling platforms. Therefore this may mean you will only sell 90 units profitably.

How To Effectively Manage The Seasonal Plan

A question you need to ask initially is very basic; what is the most likely level of sales from the stock I am going to buy (excluding any special orders) by month, week or by day. It is very important to understand the question that you have just asked yourself and realise that you are asking what is the most likely level of sales, not how many could I sell. As you could easily get into trouble if you plan the latter.

Consider the following in your seasonal sales plan: Review the prior year/s sales history. Make allowances and adjustments for unusual events such as weather, periods of out of stock issues, one off promotional sales, special orders etc.

Factoring increases or decreases based on current sales trends and the potential of sales levels for the up and coming season with a review of your competitors marketing strategies.

If you are a niche product seller check to see if there is any new competition in the marketplace that will either effect your sales or will be likely to market heavily against your own marketing strategy.

If one of the major multiples have purchased the same niche product as you try to ascertain how and where they have purchased and look at their historical sales strategy. It may be that you need to take a very uncomfortable decision and no longer sell that particular product due to the level of competitors that have come into the marketplace and squeezing the margin for profitability.

Marketing plan. In addition to having an online presence, press advertising, direct mail, media advertising how are you going to reach your potential customers? What makes you unique and different? What do you offer that your competitors do not? All these questions need to be considered when putting your marketing plan together.

Hours and staffing levels. You need to determine whether you are going to have to increase your cost base in either hours worked, temporary staff, longer hours, overnight working higher volumes of postage and packaging materials on hand to deal with the increase in sales.

Easy Ways To Plan Your Stock Levels

Once you have put your initial plans in place the next step is to build your inventory plan, the question is how much stock you will need on your shelf at any particular time, what is the continuity of supply from your supply chain, what is the opportunity to purchase additional stock levels to deal with one-off special orders, how much notice does your supplier require to ensure that they have adequate supplies in the warehouse to meet your requirements.

Plan your discounts ahead of time:

- What is your recommended retail selling price (RRP)?
- What is your launch selling price?
- What is your promotional discount selling price?
- What is your last minute reduced selling price (if required)?
- What is your clearance selling price?

Planning your discounts goes hand-in-hand with planning your sales and stock inventory and will also decide where your profit margin is going to reside in the sales cycle. Therefore you need to keep in mind that you need to protect your gross margins in your cash flow when you are doing your clearance selling prices.

You may also want to plan an early clearance if your competitors use heavy discount tactics or if weather or other unforeseen events this for the normal selling opportunity a decision will be required during the sales period that could have a major impact on your business.

Managing the sales means that you need to take regular readings of the sales and sales trends during the sales period adjusting your sales plan accordingly along with your inventory and advising suppliers accordingly on increases or decreases of your requirements. If the sales are slow or you fall behind plan make the decision and start the process of discounts early and low so that you do not end up making massive discounts all at once. Look behind the sales to get an understanding of why you may have to make markdowns, you need to be switched on and smart and asking the questions like: why is it not selling? Do the customers not like it? Is the product not visible? Is the price correct in the competitive marketplace? Is the economic climate against you? Has the lifespan of the product expired?

Always remember the customer is not necessarily looking for the cheapest price, they're looking for good value from a reputable supplier that has a good history of looking after their customers to you need to balance your sales position between perceived customer value and price.

Know Your Demographics

Understanding who your customers are in relation to specific products can be extremely useful in a similar way to that of the seasonality checklist. If your product has a target market of wealthy retired individuals, then you need to understand how those people buy products online, you may need to change the language to attract that market which could be very different to the language you would use in your sales page to attract a teenage market.

You may also want to target certain income brackets, you can obtain official statistics very easily, in the UK you would go to the Office For National Statistics, other countries will have their own version and of course you can use the Internet to obtain data.

Knowing your demographics means that you are going to start targeting people by gender, income, age, job status, family status etc. Having this information can be extremely powerful when you are putting your sales page together, so that you can target the wording of the item to that demographic that you're wanting to sell to. You may even consider putting in certain keywords or phrases either in the title or in the hidden keyword section to attract more of your desired customers.

Chapter 8 How To Use Amazon Marketing Strategies To Convert More Sales

What Is The Right Strategy For You

Picking the right marketing strategy is always going to be something of a personal preference, with Amazon you have many marketing opportunities to drive your business forward. One may be absolutely perfect for you and the others may be something to review for the future.

As Amazon's position is growing in the marketplace we are seeing them coming out with more and more strategies to help sellers compete better in the marketplace. A note of caution in that when you're looking at the marketing strategies and offer you need to be mindful of any costs involved and what that is going to do to your bottom line. They may be direct costs that Amazon are going to apply or they may be costs that you are going to incur by discounting product.

When you list an item there is a tick box that you can activate which will allow you to price your item at the lowest price against any competitor that you may be selling against on that exact same listing. This means that if the listings already in existence and you are choosing the 'sell yours here' option that lists your item immediately and competing for the buy box by ensuring your price is lower than that of your existing competitor.

If you decide to reduce your price by 1% below that of your competitor, assuming that all your metrics and customer service measurements are in good order and you meet or exceed that of your competitor you will retain the buy box (the buy box is the link in the top right-hand corner that people see and defaults to the best potential seller to deliver the item to the customer based on price and their customer service ratings and metrics).

Let us assume that during the management of your inventories you notice your competitor has now gone below or is matching your price, this may mean that your price has automatically been reduced because you have ticked the box in the listings to automatically reduce your price in line with that of your competition.

I've come across numerous items where people continue to reduce the price of an item until none of the competition are making any profit. So where you are selling mass-market products with lots of competition you need to have sound strategy to actually make the sales.

Create Huge Discounts With Sale Prices

When you list your items on Amazon, you can have up to 3 selling prices. First of all, you can have a recommended retail price (RRP). Be aware that before you discount or show a discount from the recommended retail price of your item must of been on display for a reasonable period of time at that RRP price, and if you are ever challenged you need to be able to show that it was on sale at that price for a reasonable amount of time before the discount was applied. Different countries may have different rules and regulations. Therefore please check before applying your discounts.

With Amazon with the majority of the categories you can list your recommended retail price, you are then able to list your selling price, then this may be the price that you actually want for the goods and will be your stand-alone price for selling them on a daily basis.

You may then decide to have a sale, you can plan your sales ahead by putting the start and finish dates in your spreadsheet upload or manually if you are listing one by one. This is a really useful marketing tool, as you can plan your campaigns in advance. Or if you have stock, which is not moving as quickly as you like and you have pressures of seasonality timings, you can very quickly using a separate price and quantity adjustment template make price immediate adjustments.

So let's say you have an item that has recommended retail price of £100. This is how it may look over a period of time:

- 1st of January, £100 RRP
- 1st of February, £60 normal price (40% discount)
- 1st of April sale price, £40 (60% discount)
- 1st May clearance price, £25 (75% discount)

When you use this strategy, amazon will show all of the different three price points (sale price point being the lowest) and it will also show the total value of discount the customers receiving from the original recommended retail price.

Another one of Amazon's very powerful tools in driving customers to your Amazon store.

You Can Create Marketing Campaigns

Here is another clever and currently little used opportunity to market your products in Amazon, this could be where you could really score against your competition, there are a number of campaigns that you can create and they can be driven by particular dates so that you can target in to specific events, i.e. Halloween, Christmas, Mother's Day etc.

Using this technique you can have buy one get one free, buy one get one half-price, you can tailor the campaign to suit your business strategy, one of your suppliers may come up with an offer in order to move more stock which might actually attract this type of campaign.

Currently only a few people are using the strategies, so you are in with a good chance of creating additional income or moving lines that have been sitting in your warehouse for some considerable time.

Use Fulfilment By Amazon Opportunities

You may decide that you are going to deal with your own distribution of your products, however you may have certain lines where you want to run some form of promotion as in a sale or using one of the other marketing campaigns to move stock quickly. This is where Amazon's fulfilment service may benefit you to use on an ad hoc basis.

There is no requirement for you to send all of your inventory to fulfilment by Amazon, you can just send certain lines that you want to move fairly quickly, you are now a position where you are offering free shipping, a discounted price, buy one get one half-price, for prime member's guaranteed next day delivery.

If you have good margin in this product it may be that you are using Amazon's other marketing tool which is a Amazon product adds which is a basically a pay per click service where you are paying to have your item marketed and advertised by Amazon at a small cost.

If this is the case and you are targeting customers with a very specific offer and you have a large volume of stock to move this could be very well planned and executed way of moving that stock and getting a good return on it or it may be a line of stock that you have had sitting around that hasn't moved as well as you thought and it would be a good way of turning it from dead stock with no return into cash so that at least you can go out and purchase more good quality stock.

You Can Use Amazon Product Adverts

Now this is a rather neat way of marketing from Amazon, as you do not have to have your listings already listed on Amazon or even intend to have these items listed on Amazon. There are certain criteria that you have to meet, such as opening an Amazon account, providing credit card information, having EAN numbers and SKU numbers.

You then upload your information in the required fields in the format requested by Amazon and you provide details for the adverts to be linked either to your product on Amazon or to your external website. Amazon will then attempt to match your advert with customers who are searching for similar products.

If they see your advert and click through to your product. Amazon will charge you, now you can set the maximum daily limit that Amazon can charge you and I would strongly advise you do that. Also, Amazon will advise you what the charges are per click, which will depend on the product, category and competition.

This is a brilliant way to grow your online sales on a pay per click basis, if you've already used Google shopping on Google pay per click services your have a good understanding of what you need to do to ensure that you do not overspend and that you drive the correct traffic to your listing.

Whichever marketing strategy you choose to use with Amazon you can at least be certain that Amazon is working to create buying opportunities for customers. And if you have your own marketing list that you are sending emails to with promotional offers you can link them directly to your offer on Amazon.

To be really focused on marketing strategies it could be that you will use a bundle of products (this may be an area where you have tough competition) and use a selection of the marketing techniques along with free shipping and great savings on sale price from the recommended retail price and targeted at a seasonal event, you have the makings of a great selling opportunity. You may find your suppliers will find you some very special deals so that you can move more of the product in that competitive marketplace and increase your value as a customer to that supplier.

Chapter 9 Create 'Wow' Factor Visibility, Credibility And Feedback

The Customer Is Always Right!

As far as the customer is concerned they are the most important customer in the world, the moment you start to argue with them you've lost. When you have issues, which you will, you need to accommodate them and deal with them. What you're looking for is a win-win solution. This means that both you and the customer are happy (or at least accepting of the situation).

If you argue with the customer because you know you are right you just created a win - lose situation. You win and tell everybody that listens you told that customer a thing or two! The customer loses, feels very aggrieved, leaves you negative feedback, may open a complaint case against you, and they have lost. Guess what you have also just lost a customer and some credibility.

You could go the other way, get really wound up about it, and tell the customer that they can just have what they want and they can shove it. Now you just created lose - win, you lose and feel very aggrieved, say to yourself why did I ever get into this business and the customer feels delighted that they got what they wanted when they demanded it.

Is it not better to go for a win-win solution, where both you and the customer mutually agree on the solution and you are both happy with the outcome. If your customer service is as good as that and you got every chance of making further sales to that customer and to that customer circle of friends, family and acquaintances. Not only that but they will probably leave you good feedback about your excellent customer service.

I am aware that this may cost you financially if you have to put the situation right, and it may not be an issue that you created, the fact is you need to go for win-win, not win lose and definitely not lose win.

Manage Your Customer's Expectations Under Promise And Over Deliver

When you sell an item the customer will get an anticipated delivery date from an automated email, this anticipated delivery date depends upon the settings that you put into your Amazon account (assuming you change them from the default settings when you open your account), this is of course assuming that you are using your own delivery service and not Amazons FBA services. So the rule here is make sure that all items go out on the next working day. There are times where you can to find that your items will arrive before the anticipated delivery date and its little things like that that help to get you positive feedback.

Use great packaging materials, I know we have issues around recycled and sustainable packaging, however you have also got to look at the customer's perception of what they receive. If you use old reused boxes or packaging that looks as if it has been used several times that is going to affect your feedback from that particular customer and they will feel that the item has not received the special care and attention that they would expect as a recipient. So by all means use ethically manufactured and sourced packaging but ensure that the customer receives the correct impression when they receive their item.

For those customers that purchase items and pay additional costs for expedited delivery make sure they go by next working day delivery, and that becomes so impressive that again your customer is going to leave you good feedback and potentially give you repeat business.

Manage your telephone system, if you are working from home the last thing you want is a telephone call coming through and interrupting the task that you're working on, if that is the case ensure you have a good quality answer machine and leave a very personal message inviting people to leave their contact details and let them know what time to expect a return telephone call.

When I first started out and we were busy we would leave a message on the answer machine thanking them for the call, that we were unable to take the call at that moment because we were dealing with other customers and we would phone them back after 4:00 pm that day.

This did two things, it managed their expectations of receiving the return call, it also left us enough time in the day to deal with any customer service issues if we needed to send out a replacement item or we needed to upgrade somebody from standard delivery to expedited delivery.

If you are a very large business and have an automated answering system that directs the call to the relevant department, you must ensure that those calls are rooted through extremely efficiently, if when their rooted through they go to an answer service please ensure that your customer service representative has left a personal message as outlined above. I find it extremely annoying when all I get is a message 'the person at extension 23 is not available and their mailboxes full'. Systems like that tell me that you're not customer focused or you're too big to care.

If you do have a customer service team, then you need to test your customer service. I come across many companies that believe they are doing well and never test or mystery shop their own services. If your company is big enough then test them yourself, if not ask somebody else to make a purchase and test it for you. It is advisable to test your own customer service at least 3 to 4 times per year. At least once in a very quiet trading period and then again during peak seasonal spikes where you are extremely busy. You may be surprised by your own results.

Personalise Your Email Replies

One of your measured metrics on Amazon is how quickly you respond to emails, they expect you to respond to at least 90% of inbound emails within 24 hours. If you do not achieve this target then your ratings and metrics can be affected.

I am sure you are thinking I know I will set up an auto responder, Amazon have thought of that too, messages that are sent out by an auto responder not calculated as answering the customer's email so if you use that particular method then you've still got to do a personal reply within the time period. So auto responders have a role to play in which you can help manage the customer's expectation by stating something like:

- Thank you for your email, one of our customer service team will contact you personally as soon as possible. Our offices are open Monday to Friday 9 am - 5 pm UK time. We look forward to being able to assist you and once again thank you for contacting us.

A quick auto reply like this means that the customer will have a good idea on when to expect a response, and if they're an international customer they will be able to appreciate the time zone difference.

It is also useful to compile a standard template so that you have a proportion of the email reply already completed so you only have to put in the required information that is unique to that customer's enquiry:

Thank you for your question,

I hope this answers your question and if I can be of any further assistance please do not hesitate to make contact.

I look forward to receiving and dispatching your order...

Regards

> Thank you for your email,
>
> If I can be of any further assistance please do not hesitate to make contact by email or telephone
>
> Regards

When these replies are sent out, ensure their personalised from the person who is dealing with the email, make the customer feel valued rather than signing it off 'the customer service team' it's the small details that can make the customers experience fantastic.

Where appropriate you should also provide other contact details, however always make sure your emails are rooted through the Amazon platform, this is to ensure that if there is ever any follow-up action or the Amazon customer service team needs get involved because the customer opens an A-Z case against you then you have a complete history that the Amazon representative can see so that any formal decision on A-Z cases are made with all of the factual information. More about A-Z cases in the next chapter.

Make Yourself Visible To The Customer

Customers want to feel that they are dealing with a reputable business, therefore I would advise never to use a PO Box number. This may be a personal preference issue for yourself, but most people feel more comfortable if they have an address which is real.

For those of you who are working from home, you can change part of the layout of your address by adding your company or business name so it may read 'my business Ltd, 18 the street, any town'. This will give your postal address the feel of the business.

If you feel uncomfortable with this, you can always search online for companies that will provide you with mail drop addresses in your local area, very often these are situated on business parks or services provided by high street retailers.

Making yourself visible to the customer by providing business addresses helps them feel that you are genuine. Some customers will put your address into a search engine to check you out before they buy.

If you have a genuine business address or are quite happy to use your revised home address then you need to ensure that you have registered your details with Google, it's a little bit like Yellow Pages in that if you register your business with Google and you can provide photographs of your business premises you can have an entry in the 'Google directory 'so that a small map, photograph and directions to your business will come up in a Google search.

How To Control Frequently Asked Questions

These should be a trigger for you to review your listing description all the data that you have put into your settings, if you are getting a repetitive question that means you haven't clarified or provided the necessary information. Easily fixed by revising the areas accordingly.

The description that you have placed in your sales page should answer all the questions that a customer has about product, delivery, returns, variation, colour, dimensions and measurements etc.

The truth is you are never going to answer all of their questions within the description of your product on your sales page as most people are not going to read it in full, you need to treat their question as a high priority question. It may be the simplest or considered by you the silliest question because the information is on the sales page or in the description.

Your reply needs to thank them for their question, and answer it.

Do not send a reply that says the detail is in the sales page if you would care to look. As you have just created a lose - lose situation as the customer will now decide to go elsewhere so you don't get the sale.

One of the other factors to take into consideration, and this is something that you will probably not know from the question coming in by email, is that customers educational background, their understanding of English or other language that your description has been translated to, any disabilities or visual impairments that may affect them being able to read your description.

Although you may think that it was the most ridiculous question in the world, just reflect on the fact that to that person asking the question it is very important.

If you start to receive the same question time and time again about your delivery service or a particular question regarding a product, then you need to revise and review the product or data you have submitted, it may be that you have put the detail in such a way that to customers outside of that particular industry do not understand the technical detail as it is presented. Therefore you need to find a way to change it so that they would understand it perhaps as a layman.

There is always a chance that you have forgotten to add a particular piece of very important detail into the description, so a couple of questions should trigger you to go and look at the detail and make any amendments.

If they are general questions then compile a frequently asked questions fact sheet and you can start using that to ensure that customers have access to adequate information or you can add the detail into your settings or on the product description page.

Issues Will Arise, So Fix Them

Earlier I mentioned that you should use a win-win strategy in dealing with customer issues. I have insisted in my business that my team are very customer focused. And we do whatever it takes to try make that customer feel valued and deal with their issues. Now there are some people in the world who you are never going to be able to help or to reasonably find a compromise with. They exist, deal with them and get over it.

The first thing you should do with any customer complaint is listen, find out what the complaint is about. And I advocate using the feel felt found formula:

- I know exactly how you feel Mr Smith, I have felt exactly the same way when I've had these things happen to me, what I found by doing XYZ it is rectified the problem straightaway. Now I'm sure that sounds fair to you.
- Thank you for your email, I am sorry to read the item has arrived damaged, I know how disappointed you must feel, I have spoken to my manager and I felt best thing to do is for us to send you a replacement tomorrow on the basis you can forward us photographs of the damage to the item and packaging.

    We have found that this tends to be the swiftest way to resolve problem with the least amount of inconvenience to yourself.

    If I can be of any further assistance please do not hesitate to contact me personally by email or telephone.

Responses like this are nonthreatening and they imply that you are there to assist the customer and you are making it personal to them. If you work with customers on this basis the experience I have in my business is that my customers appreciate this level of personalised service, and very often will say things like thank you very much for being so understanding, I am so pleased to speak to somebody who appreciates my predicament, don't worry about doing anything else as you have responded to my initial issue and I am more than happy with your response.

I have even had people come back to my team and say I would like to buy another one please because of your customer service. And the feedback that we can get can be brilliant. Item arrived damaged, their customer service was excellent or they solved my problem immediately. If we ignored customer service, we wouldn't have those positive inputs and the feedback would look very different from some of the customers.

Respond To All Negative Feedback

As I indicated earlier, not everybody is going to leave you positive feedback, you will get negative comments left for you and normally those are from people who cannot be bothered to make a complaint or make contact to resolve the matter as they believe that you are a large company and that is just the way it is. This one could be classed as a lose-lose situation.

So here is an example of something I would send out to somebody who was left me negative feedback, and the second one is where we have resolved the issue for the customer and they have still decided to leave negative feedback:

www.h2so.org

Thank you for your comments in your feedback, I am sorry that you didn't feel the need to contact us directly, as I felt it was a little harsh to use negative feedback when there has been no contact with us regarding the comments left. We have not been given the opportunity to deal with the issues you have raised.

All our customers have found we take customer service and satisfaction very seriously so will always look to assist with any issues... Therefore I would like to deal with the matter as a matter of urgency and ask you to revise your feedback accordingly to reflect the service all our customers enjoy.

I look forward to your reply, please do not hesitate to make contact with me personally by email or telephone

---

Thank you for your comments in your feedback, I feel it is a little harsh to use negative feedback when there has been contact between us and we refunded your item and initial postage in full.

All our customers have felt we take customer service and satisfaction very seriously so will always look to resolve any issues quickly, as we did for you.

> Therefore I am sure you found our customer service to be extremely good so I would like to invite you, as a matter of urgency, to revise your feedback accordingly to reflect the service that you and all our customers enjoy.
>
> I look forward to your confirmation of the revision, please do not hesitate to make contact with me personally by email or telephone

This type of approach very often comes complete shock and surprise to the customer, and we find in the majority of cases we are educating the customer on how the system works, a lot of the customers that will leave negative feedback are fairly new to purchasing online and believe that leaving negative feedback is the only way they are allowed to communicate with the seller.

So we tend to find that the majority of customers will work with us to resolve the problem and will also revise their feedback and remove the negative comments in their feedback. So yes this is one more process that you have to manage. You need to look at this on a regular basis so that you can be seen to be acting quickly. Do not get carried away with having your feedback open all day looking at every piece that drops in just schedule it in twice a week to check your feedback so that you can pick up on any issues.

Feedback is also a good way to check your products are reaching the customer correctly and safely as sometimes you may have accidentally mis-described an item, the chances are somebody is going to let you know this in the feedback. If that happens contact the customer thanking them for letting you know of the error send them something as a token of appreciation (if appropriate) and fix the error. If you do this you will find that that customer may agree to revise their feedback and will also be so impressed that they will buy from you again.

You have an A-Z case

A-Z cases are quite simply a method for a customer who doesn't believe that they have received standard of service that they would expect from you the seller and they're putting in a claim against you, through Amazon. It is like and internal mediation team which will look at the customers claim along with your representation in defending the claim and will make a decision based on those facts.

We find that a number of customers do not bother to make contact with us regarding their issues that go straight to an A-Z case. They are probably aware that this grabs the attention because this means that if we do not do anything about it. There is a good chance that the customer will have a full refund and we will lose the money.

Not all A-Z cases are ruled in favour of the customer, this is why I highly recommend you ensure that all communication between you the seller and your customer is completed through Amazon's internal email system. That way all of the details are there for that Amazon's team to be in possession of all of the facts.

You will have the option at the beginning of the case to offer an immediate refund, it may be that an item has been posted to the customer. They are claiming they haven't received it and it was not valuable enough for you to send it by tracked or signed delivery. Under the distant selling regulations of the customer claims they have received it and you cannot prove otherwise, you need to give them a refund or send a replacement.

If that is the case, just do it and move on. If on the other hand, you can show that the Courier delivered the item and that somebody has signed for it, then you need to be able to put all of those details to Amazon and represent your case. Amazon will then look at the details, check the tracking number and make the appropriate decision from the information they are able to obtain.

A-Z cases are there to protect both you and your customer, and if you have got a particularly awkward customer that is not trying to work with you, regardless of your efforts. There may be occasions where you will suggest to them that you are not able to help the many further, and they should open an A-Z case through Amazon.

Chapter 10 How To Understand Your Amazon Seller Ratings And Metrics

Stay Fit And Healthy As A Seller

What you need to see on your Amazon dashboard is lots of green ticks as above, this mean you're doing something correct and that your account is working for you.

Amazon look at and measure your performance against a number of areas a number of areas:

- order deficit rate
- cancellation rate
- late dispatch rate
- policy violations rate
- contact response time rate
- customer feedback scores

When you are professionally selling on Amazon you need to be aware of all of the above, and you need to be striving to achieve the highest level within the detailed ratings. These may change from time to time, so you need to ensure that you consistently stay above the minimum rating they require that each of the categories. In truth, unless you are a really bad seller. They are fairly straightforward to maintain and obtain. There may be occasions when you will slip on one of the metrics, if you do slip and you get some form of warning. Make sure you get back to where you need to be by rectifying matters.

I had an issue, some time ago when we swapped over from one piece of software to another, during the swap over a period the software managed to duplicate our sales and sent a message to Amazon, showing that our sales had not been dispatched and we received a late dispatch warning as some 280 orders overnight were reported incorrectly on the system.

That took us to a crisis position where we potentially faced our account being suspended, we resolved the software problem within a matter of hours and also contacted Amazon directly spoke to one of their account managers and although we couldn't undo the technical issue as it had happened, they were able to ensure that our account did not suffer any interruption and notes were put on for any other customer service representative to see. If you do get a problem, then deal with the problem and speak to them to ensure that they are made aware of it. So is that they can help you when necessary.

When you log into your seller account you will have a dashboard open in front of you and you can see very quickly and that dashboard. If there are any problems that need your attention. If something does arise, do not procrastinate deal with it.

Green Ticks And Red Crosses

if you have five green boxes, each with a checkmark in the, then your account is looking pretty good, if one of those green checkboxes turns orange that means that you have slipped below the minimum acceptable standard in one of those he areas.

If that checkbox goes to red with a cross in it. You have a problem. If you do not deal with whatever that problem is, and it continues to get worse. One of two things may happen, your account may be suspended or in the worst case closed. You will get plenty of warning that things aren't quite right, it is up to you to react to those warnings and deal with the issues. If you're having any problems in dealing with those issues you need to speak to their customer service team who will be able to advise how to deal with ongoing issues and rescue your position.

As I indicated earlier. It is so easy for something to go wrong and to put your account at risk.

Know The Amazon Policies

Most of the policies are fairly common sense, you are not going to sell prohibited items on the site. You are not going to mis-described miss sell or mislead customers. You are not going to sell fake items or pirate copy DVD's.

There are a range of policies that you have to adhere to, so when you start selling on Amazon, it is worth taking a couple of hours to go through the online help section which will detail all of the policies. With the best will in the world you are never going to know all of the policies, otherwise you would be working for Amazon and not on your own business, so there may be occasions where you inadvertently breach a policy.

If that happens, you need to learn from it fairly quickly, and if that breach affects any other listings that you have on Amazon you need to ensure that you deal with that breach and those listings, it may mean that you have to take them **down** and rewrite them, or it may be that there are an item that you cannot any longer sell. This may be due to you. Not having a licensing agreement, or you may be in breach of copyright, it may be that you have breach somebody's trademark without realising it. There are lots of areas where you can have an issue, and do not even know about it.

One issue we had several years ago, we had a gift product which was in the shape of a rugby ball and had the English Rugby Rose printed on the product. We received a policy violation as we had breached somebody's trademark. England Rugby Union Football Club own the trademark to the rose. They reported us to Amazon for being in breach of that trademark and having no licence to reproduce that particular rose and the item was removed from sale immediately and policy violation was awarded against us for all of the products in the range.

I would have never thought of checking to see if the rose had a trademark against it, if it had been the name of a pop star, film star, or a cartoon character, then I would have expected my supplier to have obtained permission to use the characters. Needless to say we had to withdraw that product from sale across all of our platforms and return them to our supplier for credit. They were equally surprised as they already have a number of products in the range which they have licences for. So you see it is so easy to pick up a policy violation without even knowing it.

Look Out For Policy Violation

As you have seen from the previous paragraph, you need to be looking out for potential policy violations, as if you get too many of them you may find your account is restricted.

The restriction could be a fairly minor restriction that doesn't stop you trading on a daily basis. If you get too many policy violations the restriction could be more serious in that your account could be suspended.

As I have said earlier in the worst case where you do nothing and you regularly breach policy, your account will be closed. I would have to say if this was the case, then you would probably have deserved to have the account closed as you took no action.

There is one very important piece of information that you need to be aware of, Amazon will send you emails which they will expect you to read, they will normally be regarding changes to or information about changes within Amazon's policies or procedures or notifications regarding your account and its status. If you do not click on these open them to read them, you could be in violation of policies. And these messages are always displayed on your dashboard. So there is no reason for you not to see them, however I mention this purely to ensure that you are aware that you need to look at them.

What Can You Sell On Amazon

Amazon have a number of categories which you are able to start sell in immediately, they also have a number of categories that you need to make an application to be approved to sell in, if you want to sell in one of these restricted categories you need to have built up some credibility, that credibility may be outside of Amazon and they may ask you to show where you have sold on other sites, it may be eBay or your own website.

When you apply to sell on one of these restricted sites you will be asked for various pieces of information about the products you are going to sell, you may also be asked to provide photographs, if you are please ensure that the photographs comply with their requirements.

If you have no trading history at all that you can prove to Amazon, then you will need to look at products that do not fall in those categories where you need approval and commence trading for a period of time in order to build up some credible history so that you can go back to Amazon and ask them to authorise those categories.

You Might Not Be Able To Sell Toys At Christmas

A few years ago I had a client that came to me and wanted to import toys ready for the Christmas market and sell them on Amazon. Amazon have a policy that you have to qualify every year to be able to sell toys during the Christmas period. You will need to check on Amazon's website to ensure that you have the required standard. If you do not have the required standard and you are looking to purchase toys to sell at Christmas, then you need to make the necessary changes to your account to obtain that standard to be allowed to sell toys during the Christmas period.

If you're looking at Amazon as a new venture purely to sell toys (as was the client who came to me), you will need to have built up, credibility elsewhere for them to look at your application, I would strongly suggest that you make contact with Amazon with all of your previous trading history details available so that you can discuss your position with them. This particular client decided not to take the opportunity any further thanked me for saving him many thousands of pounds which she would have potentially lost.

Chapter 11 Find Easy And Cost-Effective Ways To Ship Your Items

How Do I Cost Effectively Ship Items

One of the first things you may want to check is to ensure that you are not trying to sell prohibited items that either cannot be sent or incur special handling fees because they are classed as dangerous, hazardous or explosive. One of the things that you may have difficulty in shipping are fireworks; there are only a handful of couriers worldwide that will take anything of an explosive nature (did you know, party poppers are classed as explosives by most couriers). Liquids of any description need to be assessed first to see if they contain any chemicals that are banned from shipping or are treated in a way considered as hazardous and where specialist shipping may be required. One such item in the UK is nail polish. A small bottle of nail polish is nice, easy, light and very sellable. When you take it to the Post Office you will find that it is classed as a hazardous material and you will be charged extra as it will have to go through the Royal Mail system differently to that of general mail.

When you are looking at the items you are wanting to retail online do check a courier's exclusion/prohibited lists. You will also find on the online platforms there are items which are not permitted to be sold in eBay or Amazon; so it is well worthwhile checking the seller platform you going to use to ensure you're not going to try and sell a prohibited item. Shipping prices, postal services and courier services vary massively in the marketplace. It is a very competitive market and there are lots of people wanting to deliver your parcel to the end customer.

Simple Steps To Get Your Shipping Off To A Fine Start

Before you purchase a bulk load of products ask your wholesaler, importer, manufacturer for a finished sample of the item that you going to send as it would be packaged when it arrives with you as a stock item.

Once you have the sample product you need to decide whether it needs repackaging or whether you can just send it as it comes from the manufacturer. Packaging such as bubble wrap, void fill, boxes and mail bags are easily available online; do your research as the prices vary massively.

And don't forget to add the cost of every little bit of packaging to your overall postage cost.

Conduct a 'drop test'. If your item is potentially breakable during transit a good idea is to hold it out at arm's length approximately 1m off the floor and let it go; if it breaks or is damaged on the first drop then you need to review your packaging and the cost of your packaging materials. However if it takes numerous attempts to create damage then you've probably got a product that will get through the couriers processing system. Remember you can take all the time in the world in making your package look pretty but once it joins the thousands of packages in a courier's distribution depot it just becomes another box and will be dropped, moved from several vehicles, may go through numerous conveyor belts and then get thrown about in the back of a van on the day of delivery.

Weigh it. The very minimum you need to know is the overall packaged weight of your product once you have packaged it for posting. You need to make sure that you put everything in the package that you would put on it once it is ready to go into the postal system. If you are putting flyers, free gifts, picking notes, invoices into the package include the weight of those as well, sometimes a piece of paper weighing 10g can make all the difference between which postal rate you are going to be charged.

Measure it. Know your finished package dimensions. Then, when you are researching which postal service you're going to use, ensure that your item fits within the dimensions of the service. If not you could find yourself being penalised and having additional charges applied because your package falls into the next price banding. A number of carriers will also have restrictions on overall length - always read their small print.

Volumetric weight. If you are selling product overseas most couriers will use volumetric weight as opposed to physical dimensions, therefore it is always worth knowing your dimensions so you can put it into the volumetric weight calculator.

A courier will use a multiplication of height width and length and then create a division (this varies from carrier to carrier) to work out your volumetric weight. You will normally find that your volumetric weight is higher than the actual weight therefore the postal charge needs to be applied accordingly.

This one thing catches people out more frequently than anything else. They mis-price their international postage by applying physical weight as opposed to volumetric weight, if you do this it could cost you far more than the profit you are making on the sale.

Always try to purchase your postage online. There are lots of suppliers offering collection services or drop-off points, unless your volume is big enough to warrant opening an account. Research the online courier services and have relationships with multiple carriers to ensure you get the best deal.

Overseas postage. Ensure you get quotes from a number of different carriers or online brokers as you will find the discounts available will vary wildly from one online seller to another. Also look out for the promotion codes available when shopping for international shipping; you could easily save 5-10% by just creating a search and then leaving their web page.

If you are shipping valuable items with very high price points always ensure you use a traceable and track-able service with a signature at the point of delivery. That way you can ensure your customer has received it; some customers occasionally try to claim that they did not receive their parcel!

The above may sound all very basic or it may sound like hard work. You normally only have to measure and weigh your packaging once and if you put it into a spreadsheet or database you've got it for future reference. When prices increase or courier's options change you will be easily able to review who you are going to send your item with.

Freepost: if you are using freepost services you need to be adding your postage and packing costs to your retail price. This is perfectly acceptable on all channels, however always remember if you have a refund, loss, failed delivery, damage or other customer service related issue you will not be able to deduct the cost of the postage from the refund as no postage would have been charged in the transaction.

Therefore it is always worth adding a small margin to your postage and packing to cover such losses that will inevitably happen, regardless of how careful and diligent you are. In my business I add 2% of the retail price on all my products to cover these inevitable losses.

You also need to remember that you are responsible for the shipping of the product and for it arriving with the customer. There are no circumstances where you as the seller and shipper of the product can mitigate your responsibility to ensure that that product arrives safely with the customer.

If you try to avoid your responsibility as a seller and the customer makes a complaint to the platform you could find yourself being penalised by the platform and in the worst cases having your seller account suspended. That is why you want to be very focused on your shipping partners.

Chapter 12 Bonus Chapter: The Golden Rules To Guarantee Success Selling On Amazon

Be An Honest Seller

Lots of people dislike having to go to the car dealer, they expect to get a fairly hard sell, they assume that they are going to be sold items that they may not particularly want and be given lots of ridiculous offers that will never be available again if they buy today and sign on the dotted line of the contract.

When you are selling on Amazon, you do not need to do this, ensure that you accurately provide good quality information, do not over exaggerate claims, use factual detail.

Provide them with all of the features of the product and highlight the benefits to them of those features, if you sell two models of an item compare the features and benefits of those two models so that the customer can purchase the one that meets their needs.

I come across a few online sellers that tell me how difficult it is to sell on Amazon, how poor the customers are in making unreasonable customer service demands. An interesting fact is when I look at their offering and speak to them about their listings, the detail on their customer service procedures, I have in every case found that it is the seller that is at fault because they are not being honest seller and working within the parameters, terms and conditions that Amazon expect.

My advice is if you do not wish to work within the constraints of Amazon and provide excellent customer service to be an honest online seller, then do not go down this route as it will not be for you.

How To Stay Customer Focused

You are only as good as your last sale and your last piece of feedback. Staying customer focused can be very difficult during peak periods of business when you are juggling all of the tasks and may be against time pressure.

It is always worth taking five minutes with a cup of tea or coffee and look at where you come from in starting your online business, look at all the great pieces of feedback you have achieved. Remember some of the great conversations you've had with customers who have been delighted with your service.

It is at these times when you realise how far you have come, the changes that it is made to your lifestyle and living standards, if you are employing people then the difference it is made to their life and the fact that you putting food on the table for them and giving them a sense of purpose.

Growing an online business does have it stresses, but the rewards are excellent. I personally get a massive high out of helping other people improve their business, it really feels good when somebody comes to me and tells me they have made some changes that I have recommended and it is transformed their business.

That is one of the reasons you are reading this book, if you only implement one of the key strategies out of this book I know it will change your business. I may never know the changes that you made in your business or how the changes have affected your lifestyle but please feel free to contact me and let me know.

The Value Of A Well-Written Email

Communicating with your customers is of the massive importance, we all have really busy hectic lives and we've got to get items listed and we got a get the products sent out, you need also to scheduling time to reply to all of your emails from customers.

It is normally good to allocate time where you can be fully focused in dealing with those customer queries without anything else getting in the way.

The best way to achieve this is to set yourself some rules:

- Review all of your emails first thing before you start the other tasks to ensure that somebody hasn't sent you a request to change and address or send a different variation of the product.
- Your second review of emails may be at lunchtime.
- Your third review of emails may be towards the end of the day.

Do not let emails take over your life, they are important and they need to be responded to, the majority of customers that send those emails are realistic and are not expecting instantaneous replies.

Your email replies should be personal to the sender, personalise it by using the senders name, your sign off should always have your name appended to, along with other contact details where possible, ensure you have answered the customer's question in full or to the best of your ability.

Manage the expectations of that customer in your reply by providing them with any additional information and timeframes in relation to the enquiry and how long it may take to resolve matters if it is a customer issue.

Be Accurate In Your Product Listings

Provide good quality product listings with accurate detail, do not use too much technical jargon or if you happen to use complex technical information put into the description a 'which means' sentence that translates that technical information into either features or benefits or language that the layman will understand.

Provide the customer with all of the facts, be sure to put in dimensions of the product and the packaging along with the weight of the item. Always use metric and imperial measurements.

Use good quality keywords in your title and secondary keywords in your description, you will need to tell people what the features of your products are and then give them the benefits of those features.

Use great photography, provide as many images as you can so that they can really start to appreciate the product that they are looking at. Your pictures should have a white background where possible clean and crisp.

React To Negative Feedback Positively

Whenever you see negative feedback look at it from the positive point of view, the customer may be telling you an area where you're letting your customers down. If this is the case deal with it by fixing the area that is causing the negative feedback.

Some customers may not understand how the feedback system works correctly, so make contact with them find out what the problem is fix it and ask them to revise the feedback accordingly.

It is surprising how many customers position will change from a simple communication from you wanting obtain more information or to fix the issue that led them to leave you such negative feedback.

Do Not Take Criticism Personally

In today's world of electronic communication, people find it so much easier to be more animated, rude, forceful and aggressive when they do not have to do deal with things face-to-face or even over the telephone.

When you get these type of emails do not take it personally, they may not know of any other way of communicating, it could be they have had really bad online experiences before and this is just the last straw, it could be there just having a really bad day and you are the person that they're going to take it out on.

When you get these types of communication, stay focused the professional and do not get drawn in to an endless stream of unpleasant or offensive emails as this will just create a lose - lose situation.

Reply to them thanking them for their email or communication, use the feel, felt, found process to defuse the situation and offer to work with them and dealing with the issue. You will normally find that a response like that is so unexpected that they become apologetic for their original email or outburst to you. Very often you can turn this person into a customer for life.

Understand Amazon Want You To Succeed Too

Amazon is a great company and the great place to sell your items, customers consider Amazon as a trusted brand that gives great customer service and is easy for them to purchase products at great prices that they want.

Amazon wants great retailers who want to trade profitably and well by being customer focused, offering exceptional value for money along with fantastic customer service.

Although some commentators claim their processes are rather rigid, they work. You have to be open-minded and prepared to adapt and adopt the standards that they expect you to deliver to your customers.

You also have to do remember you are a customer to Amazon, they have an excellent customer service team for sellers, they are easily approached, they measure their customer service team's performance when you make an enquiry, they are there to help you grow your business to the levels you want in the various countries you want to trade. When you first get started you may need to contact them several times as you get used to their system. That is not a problem they have the teams in place ready to pick up and handhold you through the whole process of starting your business.

They have webinars and video instructions as well as well-written online help pages. For you to be trading on Amazon that means you are trading on one of the world's leading platforms and building up your own trusted brand.

Know Your Metrics, Ratings And Areas Of Improvement

Amazon will performance measure your business. You need to really get to understand and know your metrics, ratings and how they will affect your position within Amazon as you grow your business through Amazon.

Although it looks fairly complex, when you dig down it is fairly straightforward and is does not take long to work out where you need to be.

They are looking at your feedback scores, they will be measuring how quickly you ship items, they are measuring the number of cancellations or out of stock issues that you have had. How many customers have opened A to Z cases and make complaints against you. They want to know how quickly you are responding to emails.

You do not need to be looking at these every day, you need to be looking at your metrics on a regular basis. It will really depend on how many sales you have on Amazon to how often you need to look.

Whenever you login to your Amazon account you will be presented with a dashboard that dashboard will give you the headlines of your performance. If you see one of those performance indicators changing you need to click in and find out what the changes and where there are any issues that need addressing. Stay focused on your metrics and ratings and do not become complacent.

Delivering Great Service On Time

Over deliver and under promise, your customer needs to feel valued and your customer's expectations are that they will purchase an item from you and you will deliver it within the timeframe that they have been given.

That is all you have to do, you and I know the reality of that is there is a lot more work going on behind the scenes, but in essence that is the sum total of it. I make my purchase, I see an expected delivery time, I receive an automated dispatch email, I receive my goods.

And on the occasions things go wrong, or the customer is not satisfied just deal with it and fix it. It may cost you financially, you may need to negotiate with the customer, it may be you just have to do go that extra mile to guarantee that customer satisfaction. Then if that's what you have to do, just do it.

Delivering great service and after sales service means that your business will continue to grow, customers will return purchase more items from you, your rankings ratings will increase therefore your position in the searches will also increase, and by default your standard of living, financial wealth and your lifestyle will increase.

Selling on Amazon has definitely changed my business and also my lifestyle, it is also enabled me to help others move their businesses forward or even start businesses online. Many people asked me to write on the subject and I wondered when I would ever get the time, so now my online businesses are automated and I have a great team I have managed to fly out to a warm and sunny climate staying in five-star hotel deluxe suite watching other people sunbathe whilst I sit on the balcony writing this book for you.

Chapter 13 Bonus Page: Five Incredible Bonuses To Make Your Business Grow

As a thank you for purchasing this book I have created a number of bonuses that you can take advantage of. All you need to do is go to www.h2so.org/free-stuff **Click the link accordingly and follow the instructions.**

FREE Top 10 Amazon Mistakes And How To Avoid Them Report

FREE Chapter Of The Book On How To Sell On EBay

FREE 20 Minute Invitation For A Telephone Consultation With The Author

One Half-Price Workshop Of Your Choice

The Opportunity To Take Advantage Six Months FREE Membership To How To Sell Online When Purchasing An Annual Membership Package

Once again I would like to thank you for purchasing my book and if you ever need to contact me or my team just go to our website www.h2so.org

www.ingramcontent.com/pod-product-compliance
Lightning Source LLC
Chambersburg PA
CBHW051703170526
45167CB00002B/519